A House for Fanta

PAUL WOODS

ISBN: 1984163426
ISBN-13: 978-1984163424

DEDICATION

This book is dedicated to my wife, Fanta, in the hope that she will finally get compensation for the destruction of her house in Guinea at the hands of the wife of ex-President Lansana Conteh. It is also dedicated to the KELT colleagues, VSOs, CUSOs, Sierra Leonean lecturers, teacher supervisors, Ministry and Institute of Education officials and ordinary classroom teachers who made the time which I spent in Sierra Leone from 1981 to 1987 such a wonderful and life-changing experience.

CONTENTS

ACKNOWLEDGMENTS

Acknowledgements are due to both the sources listed as references and to the often anonymous contributors to Wikipedia who are quoted at some length, especially in relation to historical events in Sierra Leone and Guinea.

1 A MARRIAGE MADE IN MAKENI

It was the 29th of December, 1983. Although it was only seven o'clock in the morning, the sun was already burning hot in the sky above the tiny two-bedroomed bungalow at the edge of the CFAO compound in King Tom, Freetown, where I had been living for the past couple of years. A few months earlier Fanta and I had decided to get married, and today was the great day we had been planning for since August.

The wedding ceremony was to take place in the newly built Baptist church, just a few hundred metres down the road in one corner of King Tom, an island-like peninsula which jutted out into the bay. There had been some doubt about whether the church would be finished in time for the wedding. Three weeks earlier I had had a brief chat with the pastor, Moses Kanu:

"Are you quite sure that the church will be ready in time? The glass still hasn't been put in the louvre windows, there are no tiles on the floor - the whole place still looks like a building site! We still have time to move the wedding ceremony to another church or to the registry office, but we need to decide now before it's too late".

"Don't worry, Paul", Pastor Moses reassured me. It will be ready."

Not entirely convinced, we left things in the hands of God

and the Sierra Leonean workmen who were putting the finishing touches to the church building. I had paid a last minute visit to the church just the morning before, only to find the workmen were still laying the floor tiles, but they assured me they would work far into the night if they had to, and the church would be ready on time.

I had been told that it's bad luck to see your bride on the morning of your wedding, but we passed like ships in the night as I drove out of the CFAO compound looking for a petrol station which actually had petrol for sale. Freetown was in the throes of a petrol shortage and there were long queues outside the Pademba Road petrol station. I joined the tail end of the queue and resigned myself to a long wait. An hour and a half later, having persuaded them to part with a couple of gallons of petrol, I headed back to King Tom. Meanwhile Fanta, who didn't trust Mr Kai, our ageing cook, to buy the right kind of fish for the party we had planned for the evening, had gone off to the market to buy fish. I hoped she wouldn't get carried away and spend so long buying fish that there wouldn't be time to get dressed up and ready for the wedding.

Fanta's mother, aunt and sister had come for the wedding from Conakry, the capital of neighbouring Guinea, where Fanta had been brought up. The family originally came from Faranah, in the north of Guinea. Fanta's father didn't really approve of his daughter marrying a non-Muslim foreigner, but her mother, one of his four wives, had no such qualms. My parents and Aunty Joy had flown out from the UK a few days earlier, bringing the wedding cake, a three-tiered creation which had been given its own seat on the plane. When they arrived at Lungi airport, they were quizzed by a Sierra Leonean customs official.

"Why you come to Sierra Leone?"

"We're here for my son's wedding."

"Anything to declare?"

"Not really - we've brought some wedding presents, a

wedding cake and clothes. That's all."

"Have you got any weapons?" the customs man quizzed my mother.

"No, it's not a shotgun wedding," she replied.

"OK, you can go."

Relieved that they had not been asked for a "dash", they had made their way out of the arrivals lounge and we had loaded them into our waiting car, then driven them to the Cape Sierra Hotel, at the far end of Lumley Beach, which would be home for the duration of their stay. The Cape Sierra was much less grandiose than the nearby Bintumani and Mammy Yoko hotels, but much more reasonably priced.

I had invited my old friend Ralph from Brunei, now teaching in Manchester, to be the best man, repaying a debt from the time when I had been his best man when he got married to Lan in Brunei, but there was some problem with them getting tickets at the last minute. December was the height of the tourist season and he had had to pull out at short notice. Mike Foston, a VSO English teacher posted to Kabala, in the far north of Sierra Leone, came to the rescue and stepped in at the last minute to fill the breach.

Fanta had acquired an entourage of four bridesmaids: the head girl from the church choir, a policewoman who had lived next door to her in Makeni before she had moved to Freetown, and who had begged to be allowed the honour of being one of her bridesmaids, a third who was the sister of the guy we had signed up to be responsible for barbecuing the pig for the party in the evening, and the fourth Fanta's sister Marie who had come over from Conakry with her mother and aunt. The friend we had roped in to drive Fanta to the church turned up on time, and I made my way there in our now refuelled Beetle. The tiled floor looked perfect. The church was spotlessly clean and smelled quite strongly of fresh paint.

The actual wedding ceremony went without a hitch, apart from the elderly pastor to whom Moses Kanu had entrusted the task of reading out the marriage vows getting my name confused and addressing me as Richard, not Robert. Pastor Kanu preached a lively sermon about the responsibilities and perils of marriage, then we signed the marriage register.

It was the custom in Sierra Leone for everyone at the wedding to line up and sign the register, not just the key players, so there was a long hiatus whilst everyone waited to sign the book, including a couple of illiterate guests who just put their thumbprints.

Then we posed outside the church for photos, before proceeding to the Brookfields Hotel for the reception. We had invited around 100 guests, and delivered 18 cases of beer and several of sparkling wine to the hotel the day before, leaving the hotel to provide the food and soft drinks. By now the heat was taking its toll, and after the speeches and toasts we adjourned back to the CFAO compound to have a rest and get our strength up for the party in the evening.

Having started the day with four bridesmaids, however, we ended the day with only two. At some point in the proceedings Fanta noticed that the silver goblet had disappeared from the top tier of the wedding cake. A search of the house revealed that it was hidden under one of the bridesmaid's dresses where they had got changed in the spare bedroom. Fanta was convinced it could not have got there by accident and sacked the bridesmaid (her policewoman ex-neighbour from Makeni) on the spot. Shortly afterwards she noticed that a two-litre bottle of Johnnie Walker whisky which was stashed away in a cupboard along with various other bottles of hard drinks for the party in the evening appeared to have gone missing. It had to be someone in the house. Having already lost the bridesmaid who stole the silver goblet, I was anxious to avoid any further embarrassing scenes, but Fanta insisted on looking through everyone's bags and baggage.

"Here - you can look in my bag first," said my Aunty Joy, but Fanta told her not to be silly. Eventually the missing bottle was discovered in a bag belonging to the sister of the man outside in the garden who was spending the afternoon roasting the pig in readiness for the party that evening. With some difficulty I persuaded Fanta to keep quiet.

"You don't need to speak to her ever again after today, but we don't want to risk her brother taking umbrage and leaving us in the lurch with no roast pig for the party."

I don't remember much about the party. Everyone seemed to enjoy themselves. Apparently at one point I tried to take Fanta's mother for a dance. She appeared quite horrified. Nobody had told me that it's absolutely taboo in Guinean society to touch your mother-in-law.

We had a delightful time on our honeymoon, staying at the Atlantic Hotel in Banjul, the capital of the Gambia. The bedroom walls and ceiling were covered in stippled white plaster which looked just like the icing on a Christmas cake or wedding cake!

A couple of weeks later, we were back in Freetown and starting our married life together. I went along to the church to collect the marriage certificate, which I needed to send off to the British Council in London to prove we were now married and therefore entitled to additional allowances. I spent a few minutes admiring the signatures and wondering who exactly the thumb prints belonged to, then to my horror realized that, although Fanta and I had written our mothers' and fathers' names, our ages, addresses, occupations and various other personal details, where we should have signed our names, we hadn't, and the two pastors conducting the wedding had signed their names instead.

"There is a problem here", I said to Pastor Kanu.

"What problem?" he queried.

"We haven't signed the register, and the two pastors have signed it where we were supposed to sign."

"No problem. There are three copies, the one which stays in the register, the one we give to you, and the one we send to the government. We haven't sent the copy to the government yet, so we can just tear the page out of the book and start again."

"No way - we'd never be able to collect all those signatures from all the guests again."

The solution we eventually arrived at was to add "in the presence of" where the pastors had signed, then draw an arrow up to where we had signed.

The British Council quite happily accepted the altered document as proof that we were legally married and started paying the monthly marriage allowance. It wasn't a problem a decade later when our son James was born at Fazakerly Hospital in Liverpool, and the registrar issued a UK birth certificate on the strength of our Sierra Leonean marriage certificate. Several years later, when our daughter Marie was born in Brasilia, the Brazilian authorities accepted it as proof that we were legally and properly married and issued a Brazilian birth certificate for Marie. But a snag arose when I sent this off to the British Consulate in Rio de Janeiro to register Marie as a British citizen. I got a phone call from the Consul.

"We've had a look at your marriage certificate and can see that it's been altered. This means you're not legally married. If you want to register Marie's birth you'll have to go through a new marriage ceremony."

When I arrived home and reported this news to Fanta, she said,

"Well, we're not getting married all over again. We'll just have to live in sin."

A few days later there was a reception at the British Embassy in Brasilia. I happened to find myself sitting at a large round table next to the Ambassador's wife. After I'd had several glasses of the Embassy's excellent red wine, I felt sufficiently uninhibited to say to her,

"I've got a bone to pick with the Consul in Rio. He says we're not legally married."

I explained the problem with the marriage certificate. She stroked my shoulder and said,

"Don't worry about it, Paul. I'll have a word with my husband."

A few days later there was another phone call from the consulate in Rio.

"It's about your marriage certificate. We've taken another look at it, and we think it'll be o.k. So we'll issue the birth certificate you were requesting."

2 MOVING TO MAKENI

My four year stint in Tanzania working as a KELT lecturer for the British Council was coming to an end. Six months before the contract was due to finish, a consultant toured Tanzania visiting each college where we were working and produced an end-of-project report. I learned from the Council that they would be happy to re-employ us on another project, but that as our posts had been wrongly graded, it would be on a lower pay scale! The Council was in the process of moving away from the British Expatriates Supplementation Scheme (BESS), and Overseas Service Aid Scheme (OSAS),[1] where generous allowances were paid by the Overseas Development Administration (ODA) to supplement local salaries for expats on aid-related projects. Under these schemes Britain made various payments (known as inducement allowances) to top up local salaries to roughly their equivalent in the UK and also paid educational and passage allowances and gratuities to contract officers. In their place, ODA had set up the Key English Language Teaching (KELT) scheme for aid-funded English teaching, and planned to adopt a project-based approach:

"Through this scheme, ELT specialists were assigned to institutions and ministries in developing countries to deliver projects designed to reform English language teaching. Almost certainly, they were conceived of as instruments of the donors' national interests. They were also popular with the recipients' ruling elites, who saw (and continue to see) English language as an exclusive attribute carrying both prestige and material rewards.[2]

The terms and conditions for KELT lecturers were fairly generous, including a tax-free salary paid in the UK, local allowances based on the cost of living in the country, education allowances, airfares and paid annual leave. The local ministry of education was responsible for accommodation, but little else. In Tanzania each of the five KELT lecturers had been based in a college, and there wasn't much attempt officially to get us to meet together and exchange ideas and experience, never mind working on a project with specific and time-bound goals and objectives. This was all about to change.

I applied for a KELT lecturer post at the Institute of Education in Zomba, Malawi, and in reply got a letter telling me I hadn't got the post, but that the Council's Overseas Educational Appointments Department strongly advised me to apply for one of several post as KELT Lecturer in Sierra Leone. It was the first I had heard of these posts, on a new project, based in primary teachers colleges, but with a strong in-service as well as pre-service component. Thus directed, I sent in my application for a transfer to Sierra Leone.

The Sierra Leone KELT project was quite well-conceived and well-planned, but its success was contingent on a number of factors outside The British Council and ODA's control. The planning and design of the project has been described in detail by Ann Hayes, who was appointed as Ministry of Education Adviser a year in advance of other project staff.[3]. According to Hayes:

"We were lucky in Sierra Leone. We arrived on reasonably virgin soil as far as British ELT assistance was concerned; a couple of BESS English Literature teachers at the university, a handful of VSOs teaching English at secondary level, an occasional whispered mention in the odd corner of some British Council English Language Officer or other who had passed that way, or held a seminar, or presented some books, in the early seventies, or mid-sixties, or even more bygone days. There was, therefore, nothing and no one in particular to incorporate under our brief. We could start from scratch." [4]

The planning process involved answering three questions: "Why are we here?" "What can we do to achieve our aims?" and "Who will do all this?" The immediate answer to the first question was to help revitalise English teaching at primary level, primarily through teacher training at pre-service level in the five primary teacher training colleges, and at in-service level for the 7500 strong body of primary teachers, 60% of whom were unqualified and untrained, in fact only "one jump ahead of the children they purport to teach". What was needed was

- A syllabus for the schools
- Materials to realise the syllabus
- A new secondary entrance exam to reflect the syllabus
- A Teachers' College syllabus to prepare teachers in training for the above, and
- An in-service scheme to prepare serving teachers to the same end. [5]

The basic elements were already in place - the third IDA Education project aimed to prepare new syllabi and provide materials, enthusiastic TC staff worked to a syllabus based on the Institute of Education in Freetown, an EEC-funded in-service training scheme provided annual one-week courses for untrained teachers, inspectorate staff worked with admirable dedication in difficult, demoralising conditions to maintain standards, and a remarkable quantity of expertise existed in the schools, the Ministry, Institute of Education, in training colleges and in the University colleges. So the answer to question one was, "We are here to help the Sierra Leoneans in what they are already doing in ELT and coordinate their efforts." [6]

The project had three basic objectives:

- helping the Sierra Leoneans produce a new primary English syllabus and materials

- producing a new Teachers' College syllabus and ensuring in-service training reflected and supported the new school syllabus and pre-service work, and

- alerting the West African Examinations Council to changes at primary level with a view to modifying the Selective Entrance exam for secondary schools.

The intention was to provide a KELT lecturer for each of the 5 primary teachers' colleges, who would work part-time in the college and also co-ordinate a programme of in-service training courses with the Sierra Leonean teacher supervisors in each of the 16 districts. At the same time, volunteer teachers from Voluntary Service Overseas (VSO) and Canadian University Services Overseas (CUSO) would be sent to work alongside the teacher supervisors in each district. Peace Corps Volunteers were also involved in teaching in primary schools at a local level, but focused on Maths and Science, so the Peace Corps was not formally included in the project.

At the same time, the IDA was initiating a project to supply all primary schools throughout the country with over 60 textbooks covering English, Maths and Science for classes one to six. For the previous decade or more, textbooks had been almost entirely absent from Sierra Leonean schools, and teachers were lucky if they had a single copy of a book which they could laboriously copy out onto the blackboard. The Textbook Project envisaged sufficient pupils' books to be provided for pupils to share one between two, for each level of the primary school, together with accompanying teachers' books, metal cupboards for storing the books (to avoid them being stolen or eaten by rats) and a warehouse and distribution system at national and district level.

If all had gone according to plan, the textbooks would have been written and distributed coinciding with the revision of syllabuses and in-service training for the primary teachers in how to teach using books. In practice the arrival of the books was delayed and they only began to arrive in the schools towards the end of the 6-year KELT project, so for much of the time in-service training had to focus on teaching without any books!

In practice, the British Council recruited only four KELT lecturers, in addition to the Anne Hayes, the Project Leader based at the British Council office in Freetown. I was to be sent to Makeni, in the Northern Province, Judy Woodings, an experienced primary teacher trainer, was posted to the Womens' Teacher Training in Port Loko in the west, David Weir was based at Freetown Teachers' College, and Jean Conteh was at the Bo Teachers' College in the Eastern region. At the same time, ODA was funding support for Maths teaching by providing an Adviser, Pat Hughes, to be based in Freetown, Anand Nair was to be based in Makeni and Peter Poole in Bo.

Bunumbu Teachers' College, also in the east of the country, was left out of the grand scheme of things, because it was in the throes of an experiment funded by UNESCO to integrate college teaching and the rural economy. Jack Lutz, the UNESCO Advisor, co-operated closely with the KELT project but this had no direct influence on the syllabus or materials used in Bunumbu, where:

"the aim was to train "a 'new type' of teacher. With this in mind, the designers of the project included several training innovations in their writing of the project document, which is also known as a 'plan of operation'. The first of the innovations, at least in terms of primary school training programmes for Sierra Leone, was to structure a teacher-training curriculum that included the so-called 'practical subjects' and to encourage these subjects in an integrated manner. A second innovation of the Bunumbu project was an in-service training programme that emphasized curriculum development...(enabling) teachers already in the teaching service to grow professionally by participating in the writing of the curriculum they were expected to follow in their own classrooms".[7]

Identified counterparts would receive training in the UK under the Technical Cooperation Training Programme, and would work alongside the KELTs and VSOs, so that by the end of the project, envisaged for 1985, the framework would still stand, but would be totally Sierra Leonean, and the activity would be ongoing.

Ann Hayes did not anticipate that all would go like clockwork:

"At times it has all seemed to be going rather anti-clockwise, and the problems have been mainly simple human ones, for example the KELT designate who took ill, with a subsequent term's delay in filling the post; the perfect ELT teacher-supervisor designate in a provincial education office who was offered a scholarship to the University of Sierra Leone and (who can blame him?) took it. Such problems are inevitable and predictable - the difficulty of finding twelve motor-bike-riding, ELT or primary qualified VSOs; the Sierra Leonean counterparts who get trained and, when and if they can, move on to better things; the KELT who decided two years is enough for his children's health/education or his own health/career prospects; the VSO who has an unhappy love affair, or malaria (or both!). The potential problems are unlimited and mind-boggling".[8]

The first communication I received from the British Council was a brief note from Ann Hayes, the Project Adviser:

Dunford House
3rd August 1981

Dear Paul

I am writing to let you know how much we are looking forward to having you with us in Sierra Leone, and also to let you have a few details about the place, job etc. (OEAD may already have done the latter but I never <u>quite</u> trust them to send on to the relevant people the relevant bits of paper we send them for that purpose).

Firstly, the place - the Principal is marvellous, with a great sense of humour and Anglophile (well, really Scotophile, but you could add a lilt to your accent) tendencies. He's set aside a nice little flat in a modern block on campus, and as the college has its own electricity and water supplied you should be ok for mod cons. The flat is small - one bedroom, living room, tiny kitchen and a shower, but in very good condition and perfect (we think) for a single person.

Second, job - all this will be explained to you in great detail when you arrive, since we envisage a 2-3 day briefing session in Freetown for everyone. Meanwhile, I enclose a copy of my most recent report on the KELT project and this has a general outline of the job in it. Also enclosed is a draft copy of the new primary school syllabus for the IDA project that the Teachers College syllabus will have to be based on.

Best wishes,
Ann Hayes

This was followed closely by a letter from the Assistant Representative, Colin Stevenson:

Freetown 15 /9

Dear Paul
Ann has asked me to answer some of your queries. Unfortunately I've left your letter and her reply in the office, so I'll do some from memory and add a P.S. tomorrow, if I've forgotten anything important.

First, a car. That's a real problem. The following British cars are vaguely suitable: Ford Cortina, Ford Escort (old model only - no spares for the new one), BL Marina, Land Rover, Talbot Avenger. Other cars have been imported, but spares and servicing are difficult in Freetown, let alone Makeni. Foreign cars are well represented: Peugeot 504, Audi, Mercedes, various Japanese, but spares and servicing varies. Given that it will take at least two months from UK delivery to local delivery, adding on factory delay, etc, it would probably be Christmas or beyond before you see a new car. Your official KELT Land Rover may not be ready for use until November or later - it's very difficult to judge at present. You may do best, unless you particularly want a new car, to buy second-hand locally. It really depends how much travelling, outside your official duties, you intend to do. If you plan to "see Sierra Leone", you'll need a Land Rover or similar. If you don't, a new car could be an expensive luxury. That's all rather unhelpful, I'm afraid; so much depends on the travelling you intend to do. You will be living on campus in Makeni, and it's a pretty small town. You will need transport if you want to make regular private trips to Freetown. If not so regular, the express bus is good and cheap.

I wouldn't bother with a freezer. Your flat, although quite reasonable, is pretty small and you haven't got a lot of spare space. Electricity in Makeni is non-existent. The college has its own generator, but I'm not over sanguine about their supply of fuel oil to run it. We are supplying you with a kerosene fridge and a gas cooker. At this stage, we are not purchasing air conditioners from the UK for provincial posts, as there is no power. If you find you really do have electricity and want an air conditioner we will get one for you.

Television is a non-starter. The programmes are appalling and it is very difficult to pick up the signal from Freetown. I understand that, even if there is electricity, reception in Makeni is nil. Sorry!

There are periodic shortages of most things, but they appear from time to time, albeit at high prices. Bring toiletries, patent medicines/drugs, and anything you can't live without. A radio with decent shortwave is useful for the BBC world service, and a battery cassette player for tapes would be good. In fact, books and other amusements are indispensible.

I updated the "Record of Living Conditions" earlier this year but it is completely Freetown-oriented. Makeni is small, quiet and pretty backwoods. There are few Europeans, and not much social life compared to Freetown. Nonetheless, it seems a pleasant place and you're only two and a half hours away on a tarred road (with potholes). I'm sure you'll enjoy it. Before I sign off, could I ask you a favour? Our Talbot Avenger's steering is damaged and there are no spare parts available here. Could you order the following parts to be shipped out with your heavy baggage? ....

I enclose a blank cheque and hope it's not too much trouble. You don't need to specify car spares in your customs declaration - we'll sort that out in the usual West African manner when the time comes! Looking forward to meeting you soon.

Colin Stevenson
(Assistant Representative)

I spent my time usefully, reading whatever books and articles I could find about Sierra Leone. Located on the west coast of Africa, on the bulge between Liberia and Guinea, it was first "discovered" in 1460 by an intrepid Portuguese seafarer, Pedro da Cinta, who landed on the edge of the mountainous Freetown peninsula and gave it the name "Serra Lyoa", or "Lion Mountain" in Portuguese. The early history of Sierra Leone is described in a fascinating comic book (Seguin,1984) entitled, "Once Upon a Time Sierra Leone..... and a President Called Siaka Stevens"[9], an unashamedly propagandist and populist account of post-independence Sierra Leone published shortly before Stevens handed over the reins of power to President Joseph Momoh, then retired into obscurity to write his autobiography, "What Life Has Taught Me". [10]

According to Seguin, people lived in this part of Africa at least 2500 years before Christ, making simple stone chopping tools which they used for skinning animals and wood working. With no knowledge of iron, pottery-making or agriculture, they lived by fishing, hunting and collecting roots and fruits. By 600 A.D. they had discovered iron and were making highly decorated pots which were much more elaborate than the country pots of today. Eight centuries later, Portuguese explorers described several major tribes: Temnes, Mendes, Bulloms, Susu, Vai, Kono, Koranko and Yalunka.

"Society was polygamous and a man had as many wives as he could pay the bride-price for. Poro was the young men's initiation into adulthood. They were secluded in isolated areas in the bush for two years. They were taught the songs of adulthood and the arts of war and the role of adults in society and the laws ruling the daily life." [11]

The Portuguese soon began to engage in the ivory trade, but the Englishman John Hawkins had other plans and in 1562 took the first cargo of slaves from Sierra Leone. Europeans then began visiting the coast more frequently to obtain slaves, who were often captured during local wars between the different tribes, who were being supplied with guns by the Europeans.

In 1605 a Jesuit priest, Father Barreira, arrived in Freetown and succeeded in baptizing several African chiefs. But Islam was advancing southwards and in 1727 a jihad or holy war took place in Futa Jallon, around the present north-east border with Guinea.

"The jihad was a success and a strong Islamic government was established over the Yalunka country. Thus Islam entered

Sierra Leone, sometimes by war-like, more often by peaceful means.

In 1772 Lord Chief Justice Mansfield declared slavery illegal in Great Britain. By the end of the year, there were more than 15,000 ex-slaves in London alone...."[12]

Five years later, Sir Granville Sharpe got permission to found a colony for freed slaves in Africa, and in 1787 Captain Thompson bought a piece of land from a local chief, Naimbana. Soon the first contingent of freed slaves arrived and in 1792 Freetown was founded. 1190 freed slaves from Nova Scotia arrived shortly afterwards, and in 1800 a group of Maroons from Jamaica helped the settlers to defeat the local chiefs. Most of the early settlers died; those that escaped diseases such as malaria and bilharzia were invariably killed off by the indigenous inhabitants.

In 1807 Britain outlawed the slave trade and passed a law allowing British naval vessels to capture slave ships. The slaves they set free, known as "re-captives", were settled in Freetown, and in 1808 the Province of Freedom became a British crown colony. By 1850 over 40,000 re-captives had been settled in Sierra Leone, first trading timber, then later growing groundnuts. Charles Heddle, known as "the groundnut king", became the largest merchant in the colony.

Following the Congress of Berlin in 1884, the "scramble for Africa" began in earnest. In 1896 the British government created a frontier police to protect the interests of the colony from the French, and also proclaimed a protectorate over the interior, signing treaties of friendship with the local chiefs. Then in 1898 the colonial government imposed a hut tax to provide funds for administration, which sparked off Bai Bureh's six month long but abortive revolt.

On the 24th of August 1905 in Moyamba, Sergeant James Stevens' wife gave birth to a son. He was given the name Siaka Probyn Stephens, after a British governor named Probyn under whom Stevens' father served several years earlier. Seguin describes the birth and early years of Siaka Stevens and his rise to power within the All Peoples Congress party (APC).

"Born in Mende land, young Siaka hails from a Limba father and a Gallines mother. This family background will lead him to be a true nationalist".[13] Siaka Stevens is educated at the UBC school in Moyamba, and is only 9 years old when the first world war starts. As victory comes, Siaka Stevens is in Freetown studying at the Albert Academy. In 1923 he joins the Sierra Leone police, then later becomes Secretary-General of the Mine Workers Union:

"securing considerable improvement in wages and working conditions for more than 7000 mine workers. In 1931, a prominent Sierra Leonean citizen, Isaac Wallace-Johnson, organises an African workers' union in Lagos, Nigeria. Seven years later he returns to Sierra Leone, where he launches the West Africa Youth League, making a name for himself as a champion of workers' protest." [14]

On the outbreak of war in 1939, Wallace Johnson was sentenced to imprisonment with hard labour, then in 1944, as victory approached, the league leaders were all released.

In 1947 Siaka Stevens spent a year at Ruskin College in Oxford studying trade unionism and industrial relations, then on his return home was elected to the Legislative Assembly. In 1951 he became the first Minister of Mines and Labour. In 1957 universal adult suffrage was introduced and Milton Margai's Sierra Leone Peoples' Party (SLPP) won the elections. His brother Albert Margai felt progress towards independence was too slow, and in 1958 Albert Margai and Siaka Stevens formed the Peoples' National Party (PNP) to press for independence and African control of the civil service and industry. A constitutional conference was called in London and April 27th 1961 was selected as the date for independence. However, Siaka Stevens refused to sign the independence documents and launched an "elections before independence" movement. This became the All Peoples' Congress movement (APC).

Fearing violence during the independence celebrations, the Prime Minister, Sir Milton Margai, had Siaka Stevens along with 43 other leaders thrown into jail a month before the Independence Day celebrations. In 1964 Milton Margai died and was replaced as Prime Minister by his brother Albert. The SLPP proposed a one-party state, causing a strong reaction from the APC, who won the 1967 general election. This was followed by social unrest and a military takeover.

In 1968 the country returned to civilian rule, and Siaka Stevens came back from exile to form a government, and was sworn in as Prime Minister.

In 1971 Sierra Leone became a republic and Siaka Stevens was sworn in as the first president, for a 5-year term. To quote Seguin,

"Under APC and Dr Stevens' government, progress and development start in every field.... Feb 15 1973 - the country's first national commercial bank...is formally opened by the President. May 9, 1973 - figures are published revealing considerable economic growth since the APC took office... statistics also demonstrate marked improvement in educational and health facilities." [15]

In March 1976 President Stevens was unanimously re-elected President for the next five years, then in the May 1977 elections the APC won a landslide victory with 74 seats, with the SLPP winning only 15 seats and others 3 seats. Spurred on by this victory in June 1978, after a week-long referendum showing 95% support for a one-party system, Sierra Leone became a one-party state under the banner of the All Peoples' Congress, and a week later President Stevens took the oath as President for a further term of seven years. In July 1980 the OAU summit was held in Freetown and President Stevens was unanimously elected Chairman of the OAU for 1980-81, then the following year was elected Chairman of ECOWAS for 1981-

2. Seguin concludes, somewhat ironically in the light of what was to happen just a few years later:

"So was Sierra Leone, and so she is today and tomorrow...Sierra Leone will be like Sierra Leoneans ever made her: a friendly and peaceful place. As Amnesty International recently mentioned in a world-wide study on torture, Sierra Leone is one of the very few countries in the world absolutely free from the slightest attempt on human rights. Peace in the air, amazing beauty of sunset, as many Sierra Leoneans after a hard day's work.... President Stevens enjoys a drive along the ocean. "How de bodi, Pa Shaki?" "De bodi fine!" Then he goes home with his beloved family. When relaxing, he is a man of great wit and humour. He has a joke for each age group. His children say God never had been kinder than giving such a father, he loves them as much as they love him. Our lady of state put it simply, "I am in him, and him in me." Long live Sierra Leone!! Long live...Siaka Stevens!" [16]

Not every commentator is so generous. Emily Joy, who worked as a volunteer doctor in Serabu, just before the outbreak of the civil war in the '90s, has this to say:

"Siaka Stevens and his Swiss bank account did very nicely. So nicely that there was not a single railway line, power station or up-country telephone remaining when he retired thirty years later. Nor was there any opposition (opposition having been conveniently outlawed, murdered or executed) to his hand-picked successor, Major General Momoh, commander of the armed forces. Momoh made his own fortune from the British, the Lebanese and various others with rich pale skins, by coming to an agreement whereby they could help themselves to the gold and the diamonds and the rutile and the bauxite, without having to worry too much about little inconveniences like tax. Meanwhile the tribes that made up the four million strong population of Sierra Leone continued to scrape an existence off the land." [17]

3 MAKENI TEACHERS' COLLEGE

I had hoped to take a couple of months off before starting my new job in Sierra Leone, but Ann Hayes was quite insistent she wanted me there within the next three weeks in good time for the start of the college term. So I embarked on a flurry of activity, buying essential supplies to send as "heavy baggage", having numerous injections and boosters for typhoid, tetanus, cholera, yellow fever and hepatitis, stocking up with a year's supply of antimalarial pills and saying hello then goodbye in rapid succession to family and friends.

The flight out to Sierra Leone was uneventful and I was met early in the morning at Lungi airport by Anne Hayes. She was a hard-bitten, single, strong-minded Scot, in her mid-30s, who had braved the male-dominated preserve which was then the British Council's Overseas Career Service to carve out a career for herself in Teaching English overseas. She had acquired a reputation for standing for no nonsense and one poor unfortunate KELT who had arrived several months earlier had already got on the wrong side of her. His two-year contract was terminated after six months and he was sent packing.

In the early 80s, Freetown could only be reached from the airport by ferry, which had lots of atmosphere but was exhausting after a long flight, though nowadays there are several other options, including six hours by the road from

Lungi to Freetown, newly built by the Chinese, by hovercraft to Aberdeen in West Freetown, by speedboat to Kissi or Aberdeen or by narrow, open wood boats with outboard motors - cheap and crowded with about 20 - 30 locals sitting on wood seats, but quicker than the ferry.

For a time in the late 80s/early 90s, you could go by helicopter, but following a crash in 2007 which killed 22 people including the Togolese football team, these flights were suspended. The Russian pilots jumped out just before the crash. The helicopter caught fire upon impact and was destroyed before fire fighters were able to extinguish the flames. According to witnesses fire fighters did not arrive at the scene until 40 minutes after the crash. The fire fighter who had the keys to the fire truck was not at his station in the airport at the time, and airport staff had to douse the flames with buckets of water. [18]

There was a mad dash to get to the ferry, about thirty minutes' drive away, then a four hour wait until the ferry arrived and was fully loaded, followed by around ninety minutes actually on the ferry to get to Freetown on the opposite side of the bay. In fact, the journey from the airport to the centre of Freetown took roughly the same time as the flight from Heathrow to Lungi!

The British Council had arranged for me to stay for several days in Freetown at the Paramount Hotel, just down the road from the British Council office on Tower Hill. This was comfortable enough and after the chronic shortages of Tanzania the shops appeared to be well stocked with all the essentials needed for survival. I bought far more supplies than I really needed (in case they weren't available in Makeni), although Ann assured me there would be several "supermarkets" which had most things in stock. I also took the opportunity to explore the area around the Paramount Hotel, including the famous Cotton Tree, symbol of emancipation, which is said to have played a key role in the city's history when poor black settlers rested in its shadows after landing in Freetown in 1787. State House, up on Tower Hill near the Council office, with its Krio architecture, featuring brightly washed buildings and higgledy-piggledy window frames, incorporates the bastions and lion gate from Fort Thornton (built at the turn of the 19th century). The British Council office itself, built in the 1950s, had a large auditorium which was in great demand for amateur dramatics etc, and had a well-stocked library. I was also taken for a drive along Lumley Beach to the promontory where the three main tourist hotels were located, and paid a visit to Alex's Beach Bar, a well-known haunt for both locals and expats owned by a Russian who, together with his two brothers, had jumped ship in Freetown and stayed ever since. All three brothers opened bars cum restaurants and Alex's, El Ancla and the Cape Club had very similar menus. Sadly the restaurant closed a couple of years ago, but prior to its closure an enthusiastic reviewer on Trip Advisor wrote:

"Is it the best restaurant in the world? Quite possibly. First, the location overlooking the wreck of Alex's yacht shipwrecked on a voyage back from South Africa in the 80s in a beautiful crescent-shaped cove. Then the food. Preposterously large lobsters for unfeasibly low prices. Then the company. Alex himself. The shipping fraternity, hardened by years of coups and full of hair-raising stories from the bad old days. The water lapping at your feet. The cicadas on full volume. Sand between your toes. The stuff of memories".[19]

Then it was time to load my suitcase and boxes of supplies into the back of the British Council Land Rover and head northwards to Makeni. Once you left the outskirts of Freetown behind at Waterloo, the road was fairly narrow and potholed, until about half way to Makeni near Lunsar, where it was transformed into a brand new two lane super-highway, only recently completed, and yet to develop potholes. Only a few small villages along the way house more than a few hundred people, and these are mainly to be found at the junctions where roads branch off towards Port Loko, Bo and Kenema. Makeni is located where the lowlands meet the hills that rise northwards towards the border with Guinea. Overlooking the town are the twin peaks of the Wusum and Mena hills, named after the husband and wife devils, who are said to live on them. Makeni is the fourth largest town in the country. After two and a half hours, around lunch time, we reached the turnoff to Makeni town, marked by a BP petrol station and a footbridge over the main road. Another couple of miles along the superhighway we arrived at the beige-coloured walls of Makeni Teachers College, fringed by iron railings. After a brief stop at the college office, where I was introduced to the Principal, Dr. J. S. Lenga-Kroma, who had gained his Doctorate from Edinburgh University, by writing his thesis on a history of the Southern Temne, I was escorted to the flat which was to be home for the next 18 months. This was on the ground floor of a three-storey blocks of flats, close to the main entrance to the college. My goods and chattels offloaded, Ann said a brief farewell as she was anxious to get back to Freetown by mid-afternoon. The flat looked habitable enough, apart from a metal bedstead with sagging springs and a metal bar across the middle of the frame which looked highly uncomfortable to sleep on. The fridge and cooker had been delivered earlier by a British Council driver and seemed to be in good working order. Ann said her goodbyes and drove off. I then had a few moments of regret, wondering what on earth I had let myself in for, but these soon passed.

The College was founded in 1964 by the Catholic Diocese of Makeni, as the St. Augustine's Teacher's College, as a step towards improving education for the formation of primary school teachers many of whom were unqualified. The archdiocese spent a great deal on building a new college, with staff accommodation, spacious classrooms and student dormitories, and shortly after this was completed it was taken over by the government. The name was changed to the Makeni

Teachers College, and now it was offering two year Higher Teachers Certificate and three-year Teachers Certificate courses. English was one of the key subjects on the primary curriculum in all the schools, but the standard was pretty low, as the teachers own qualifications were limited, teachers were often unqualified and unpaid for long periods, and there was a general lack of books and materials for teaching.

"The college was upgraded, through the Polytechnics Act of 2001, to the Northern Polytechnic, incorporating the Islamic College Magburaka and the Magburaka Trade Centre. Since 2004, it has resumed operations in Makeni after the rebel war. The student population is currently about 1,000. Programmes offered include the Teacher's Certificate and Higher Teacher's Certificate, with courses in agriculture, practical and creative arts, home sciences and others." [20]

4 THE FIRST TERM IN MAKENI

Despite the British Council's rush to get me to Makeni, teaching did not commence for several weeks as the students were still on holiday. John Conteh, our Head of the English Department, assigned me the job of reviewing and revising the English syllabus and teaching programme for the Higher Teachers Certificate students - a fairly daunting task. I also got to know Makeni town and found things to keep me occupied in my free time. I did my shopping in the market, or in one or other of the Lebanese-owned shops near the town centre. Makeni's market, as described by Gearoid Millar, is:

"a dimly lit hubbub of humanity that has changed little with time. Here young girls and boys work alongside a few men and hundreds of women to sell scores of local staples, from groundnut paste and cassava leaves to rice and beans, locally made shampoo and soap to salt and sugar. At the market some women sit slumped on a half-empty sack of rice or an upturned crate, no longer bothering to try to attract customers, while others cry out their wares and their prices over the din of competing cries and the noise of children playing among the stalls or babies sitting on top of a table here, under a table there. In the market, young children - sometimes just 5 or 6 years old - proceed from person to person trying to sell dried fish, pieces of hotdog on toothpicks, hard candies, plastic bags or any number of other cheap provisions. Here you can often see women barely able to remain awake, exhausted perhaps by the heat, the noise, typhoid, malaria, or some combination of them all. At the lower end of the market... you could find a massive pile of waste, swarming with flies and stinking of decay, around which yet more women sat selling their wares, often edible provisions such as beans, rice, fish, cassava and eggs, and on which the flies swirled. In this way, while the market is a site of commerce and activity, it is also a place where a visitor can see those left behind by progress and development". [21]

The college day started early and ended early, and by 4.30 or so I often made my way along to the Tennis Club, a single hard court where the same group of ageing Lebanese traders used to meet every afternoon. I was somewhat outclassed but usually managed to find someone who was about my level to play against. One of the regulars was Dr Kamara, who worked at the local government hospital and had spent several years in Russia getting his degree, whilst in the process falling in love with an attractive Russian girl, probably in her thirties, who must have been bored out of her mind in Makeni and was slowly drinking herself to death on vodka. Sadly her liver gave out and she passed away not long before I moved to Freetown.

On Sunday mornings I would make my way to the Baptist church, a short distance along the road towards Lunsar. In a letter to my parents, I described how:

"last Sunday I had to preach the sermon. Someone translated it into Krio for the benefit of the non-English speakers. I also play the organ for them now on Sundays. They have an ancient Sally Army style harmonium powered by foot pedals and when they found out I could play hymns passably, I got roped in as the organist. On the odd occasions when the town electricity supply is on, I take my keyboard along, because you don't have to peddle like fury to get any sound out of it!"

I soon discovered quite soon that the expatriate population of Makeni was limited to a few priests and nuns, various old established Lebanese shopkeepers, who were by now de facto Sierra Leoneans, and an agriculturalist working for the Agriculture Ministry who was getting very frustrated because his agency was refusing to finance a scheme to rear "cutting grass" commercially. (A cutting grass, or cane rat, is a very large rodent about the size of a small pig which is very tasty when eaten with rice and hot pepper sauce). Apparently the powers that be had decided they couldn't support the idea of feeding humans on rats. According to Wikipedia:

"In the savanna area of West Africa, people have traditionally captured wild cane rats and fattened them in captivity. More recently, intensive production of cane rats has been undertaken in countries such as Benin and Togo and agricultural extension services in Cameroon, Côte d'Ivoire, Gabon, Ghana, Nigeria, Senegal, and the Democratic Republic of Congo have also encouraged farmers to rear these rodents in rural and peri-urban areas. Research carried out over the last two decades has allowed the selection and improvement of stock for captivity and much of the knowledge and techniques for cane rat breeding has been determined from work carried out at the Benin-Germany breeding station, which was established in the mid-1980s." [22]

It seems he was way ahead of his time.

There were also several VSO volunteers, including Kevin Cresswell, a cockney mechanic from the East End of London whose speech was liberally peppered with "f***" and "f******". He maintained vehicles and did other odd jobs for the Catholic mission and lived in a small rented house with the designation "The Queen's Thighs" painted over the gateway. There were three other VSOs, working for the Ministry of Works, and most afternoons after work the VSOs could be found at Mrs Kargbo's bar, which was also popular with visiting Peace Corps volunteers.

VSO had organised a week-long Temne course in Freetown for newly arrived volunteers posted to the northern province. Temne is one of 16 indigenous languages spoken in Sierra Leone and is used mainly in the Northern Province. I managed to persuade the British Council that it would be useful for me to attend this as part of my job would involve travelling around the province visiting and supporting the local teacher supervisors for English, who were to be joined in a few months' time by VSO English teachers who would be responsible running in-service training workshops at district level. However, as virtually everyone I worked with spoke English and those who didn't spoke the national lingua franca, Krio, I forgot what I had learnt almost immediately, as there was little chance to practice.

Krio is, as the name suggests, the creole language which developed as a result of contact between the early settlers and the local indigenous tribes. According to Wikipedia, it:

"is spoken by 97% of Sierra Leone's population and unites the different ethnic groups in the country, especially in their trade and social interaction with each other. Krio is the primary language of communication among Sierra Leoneans at home and abroad. The language is native to the Sierra Leone Creole people or Krios, (a community of about 300,000 descendants of freed slaves from the West Indies, United States and the British Empire), and is spoken as a second language by millions of other Sierra Leoneans belonging to the country's indigenous tribes. English is Sierra Leone's official language, while Krio, despite its common use throughout the country, has no official status." [23]

While in Freetown I looked around for a suitable car. If you wanted a car loan from The British Council you had to buy a British made car. After my disastrous experiences with a Chrysler (Talbot) Avenger in Tanzania, and seeing the difficulties people like Colin Stevenson were experiencing trying to keep a British-made car on the road in Sierra Leone, I decided to go for a locally-purchased car which could withstand the rigours of the Sierra Leone road system, and to forego the benefits of an interest-free car loan. After shopping around looking at Toyotas, Peugeots and other makes suitable for awful roads, I finally came down in favour of a Brazilian-made Volkswagen Beetle from Brewo Motors. This had the advantage of having a pretty simple engine, mounted at the rear in what would normally have been the car boot, and spare parts appeared to be easily available at reasonable prices. (In fact, the Beetle was to serve me well for the six years I spent in Sierra Leone, until the engine caught fire the month before I was due to leave.) There was an amusing incident the next year, when I was on my way in the Beetle to Bo, and got flagged down at a roadblock manned by several soldiers who looked as if they were either drunk or high on drugs.

"Kushe-o." (Hello.)

"Kushe."

"Ow de bodi?" (How are you?)

"De bodi wehl." (Fine, thank you)

"Usaid yu komoht? (Where are you from?)

"Makeni."

"Usaid yu de go? (Where are you going to?)

"Ah de go Bo." (I'm going to Bo.)

"Ah get foh see yu lisens. (Show me your licence.)

I rooted around in my bag and found my licence. So far, so good. Then they asked for my insurance. I searched around in the glove compartment but all I could find was a cover note, valid for a month, dating back to when I had bought the car a year earlier. I was starting to get a bit worried. Next they demanded to see the vehicle log book with the registration details. I knew I had that, so pulled it out of the glove compartment with a flourish. One of the soldiers examined the document at some length. Then he walked round to the front of the car. After re-examining the log book he walked round to the rear. Then, "Why yu don change yu number? (Why have you changed your number?)

Guessing he was probably illiterate, I grabbed the registration book and checked the number, only to discover that the number plates must have been painted by a dyslexic sign-writer. The number in the book was quite clearly stated as WU12578 but the numbers on both the number plates were WU 87521. I resigned myself to my fate.

"Wi no get foh eat." (We need something to eat.)

Not fancying being carried off to the nearest police post or worse, I surreptitiously delved into my wallet, pulled out a fistful of 100 Leone notes and stuffed them into the soldier's outstretched palm.

"Tell God tengki, Wi go see." (Thank God. See you again.) And with that he raised the barrier and off I drove. It turned out on close examination that the numbers were not painted onto the plates, but were made of a kind of self-adhesive white plastic, so it was comparatively easy to remove them and stick them back in the right order.

Several years earlier, halfway through my three-year contract in Brunei, I had broken off the only meaningful long-term relationship I had ever formed, with Helen, a nurse I had met whilst doing teaching practice in Bristol. It hadn't survived the long distance separation. Then for four years in Tanzania I had lived in two small provincial towns where the chances of meeting your life partner were pretty remote. Not long after arriving in Makeni one of the other lecturers, Mr Luseni, had introduced me to Mary Coker, a student teacher at Milton Margai Teachers' College in Freetown, but this relationship wasn't going anywhere. Now over thirty, I had the feeling I ought to be thinking about getting married, settling down, having a family, but it didn't look as if this was going to happen any time soon, at least not in Makeni!

For most people in Makeni, life was something of a struggle. As Millar points out:

"while the houses in Makeni are of a regular, relatively simple style, they vary greatly in their quality and state of repair. Regularly a bare unpainted block house, with wooden shutters instead of glass windows, sheets for curtains instead of doors, and patched leaking zinc (corrugated iron) roof, will stand next to or across the street from a newly refurbished house with glass windows, solid wood or metal doors, whole or even new zinc, and level, solid concrete floors and walls. These are the inequalities of any town, but they are made more evident by the extreme poverty of many lives in Makeni." [24]

Millar also describes the lorry parks, the larger of which is in the town centre on Rogbani Road, and a smaller one near the NP (formerly BP) petrol station where the Freetown highway enters the town:

"At both of these lorry parks the press of humanity attempting to cram into taxis, poda podas (minibuses) and onto the backs or even the roofs of trucks and cars, reminds visitors that ... most people are not enjoying the benefits of progress but are continuing to struggle through life, day by day. At both of these sites young men and women run eagerly to every window of every vehicle begging for someone to buy their cassava, roasted meat, bread, boiled eggs, or whatever else they carry on their heads all day, hoping desperately to earn their day's chop (food). It is here too that a visitor can witness interaction between the elite Sierra Leoneans and expatriates in late-model Land-Rovers and the average Sierra Leonean; that of a quick unequal economic exchange; of unquestioned superiority and obsequious deference". [25]

For most Makeni residents, life goes on pretty much as it has always done:

"It is here that children roam around in their underwear or take their baths in buckets of water in front of the house, boys congregate and play football barefoot or in much patched plastic sandals, tired men sit drinking attire (Chinese tea) and poyo (palm wine) and discuss the issues of the day, and women

young and old talk, prepare dinner and keep children in line."
(26)

5 CHRISTMAS DAY 1981

I had survived the first term, which once it got started was actually quite short. The college campus was now pretty much deserted, the students had all returned home for the Christmas holidays, and the weather was hot, dry and somewhat oppressive. Christmas Day fell on a Friday, and Kevin and I had been invited for Christmas lunch with turkey, Christmas pudding and all the trimmings by some expats who lived beyond Magburaka. We had a thoroughly enjoyable lunch and arrived back in Makeni towards evening. I guess Mrs Kargbo's bar was probably closed for Christmas, and so, having had a lengthy siesta to sleep off the effects of lunch, and being at a loose end later in the evening with nothing else to do, we ended up, slightly the worse for wear, at a dance at the Teko army barracks. This was a bit sleazy, with drunken soldiers vastly outnumbering the small number of women brave enough to venture along to the barracks, and by the small hours of the morning we had had enough of dancing. But loathe to head for bed, we decided to have a final drink at the BP petrol station. The petrol station, at the turning off the main road into Makeni town, had a small bar with six or seven tables and was a good alternative to Mrs Kargbo's.

A few late night revellers were sitting at the other tables, most of them drinking Star beer. I noticed a very striking girl, apparently on her own, who was sitting on a high stool at the bar drinking Fanta. She was dressed in a long white dress which came down below the knee, decorated with a single red heart. Kevin knew just about every pretty girl in Makeni , so I turned to him and asked,

"Who's she? Looks like she's just sitting there on her own."

"No idea," replied Kevin. "Never seen her before in my life."

The fact that Kevin didn't know who she was suggested that perhaps she was not necessarily the kind of girl you were likely to find in a Makeni bar at 3.00 a.m. on Boxing Day morning. After downing another beer, I plucked up the courage to go over and say,

"Hello there. I'm Paul. Could I buy you a drink?"

Looking at me somewhat disdainfully, she replied in a French-sounding accent, "I'm sorry, I don't accept drinks from strangers."

I retreated back to the table where Kevin and I were sitting. After a few minutes a girl he knew came over and joined us. Still curious about the girl in white on the bar-stool, I asked if she knew who this girl was.

"She's from Guinea. I think her name's Fatmata."

Kevin said, "You should go over and ask her to join us. Paul wants to buy her a drink."

I guess she must have decided there was safety in numbers and somewhat reluctantly came over, sat down at our table and finally accepted my offer to buy her another drink. It turned out everyone called her Fanta for short, and she was a Guinean from Conakry who was working as a French-speaking secretary for Fougerolle, the French company which was building the new road north of Makeni towards Kabala. Her English was pretty basic, and I had never studied French at school, having started with German and then done Russian at "A" level. But we managed to get by in a mixture of English, French and Krio.

Around 4.00 a.m. we all decided it was time to head for home. We had planned to go for a picnic the next day to Bumbuna, where there was said to be a pretty waterfall, and to my delight Fanta agreed to come along too.

Bumbuna, on the Seli River, where the river flows through a gorge below some impressive falls is now the location of a major hydroelectric power scheme. Construction had started on a dam in the mid seventies, but little progress had been made.

"The plant ... was built over a period of 35 years. It produces 35MW and was intended to provide consistent, inexpensive and clean energy for the region. Insufficient water supply to the Bumbuna dam and technical problems contributed to low production. The first phase of the project was completed and commissioned in November 2009. It was launched to provide a consistent, inexpensive and clean source of energy for the region .... The Bumbuna dam is 88m high and 400m long. Two tunnels run on the right and left side of the dam. The left tunnel is used as the primary spillway while the right tunnel functions as the power tunnel and auxiliary spillway. The intake for the right tunnel is a 93m concrete tower with a diameter of 7.5m.

In May 2011, the government of Sierra Leone signed an agreement with US-based Joule Africa to undertake the plant's second phase of development." [21] This phase was expected to cost US$750m and to be completed by 2017. However progress was slow and only in July 2017 was it reported that Joule Africa and the government of Sierra Leone had signed a 25-year power purchase agreement for electricity from a 143-MW expansion of the 50-MW Bumbuna station. This expansion, called Bumbuna II, was to be located on the Upper Seli River in the northeast part of the country, about 30 miles north of the existing Bumbuna scheme. Construction was expected to start by mid-2018, with operations to begin four years later. Henry Macauley, the Minister of Energy said:

"This is a critical project for Sierra Leone and represents an important step in helping to resolve our country's power deficit. When operational, Bumbuna II will make the most of harnessing and managing Sierra Leone's heavy, seasonal rainfall and will provide clean, reliable energy for generations to come." [22]

6 SCALING MT BINTUMANI

The second term passed uneventfully, and during the Easter holidays I made plans to scale Mt. Bintumani, the highest mountain in West Africa, accompanied by a couple of VSO teachers. Having previously conquered Mt Kilimanjaro, the highest mountain in Africa, and Mt Kinabalu, the highest in South East Asia, I expected Mt Bintumani to be a piece of cake. Knowing that the roads were likely to be pretty atrocious, I decided that, rather than taking the Beetle to the starting point at Yiffin, it would be best to go in the British Council Land Rover. That way, if we got stuck in deep mud or had to ford rivers and streams with no bridges we at least stood a chance of avoiding disaster. From Makeni we went north up the tarred road to Kabala, where we picked up our third intrepid climber, then set off south-eastwards on the dirt road to Yiffin.

To add to the element of danger, Sierra Leone was holding hotly contested elections the following month. The British Council had sent round a circular a few weeks before, warning of the risk of spontaneous pre-election violence and advising against travelling anywhere during the Easter holidays.

"If they think I'm going to spend two and half weeks twiddling my thumbs in Makeni, they can have another think", I told Kevin one afternoon in Mrs Kargbo's bar as we speculated on whether the British Council was just being over-cautious.

The journey from Kabala to Yiffin took about six hours down what must be one of the worst roads in Sierra Leone, with potholed laterite and gravel interspersed with good stretches with terrible corrugations, passing through small villages of mud-brick cottages with grass roofs, the odd goat or chicken dashing across the road, women in brightly coloured cloths pounding yams and crushing chillies for the next meal, and wide eyed kids shouting slogans as we passed. In one village we came across a grey-painted Land Rover which looked almost identical to ours, except for "Electoral Commission" painted on the front doors, rather than "KELT Project," whilst in another village the burnt-out remains of what might well have been a Land Rover belonging to the Electoral Commission could be seen at the edge of a small ravine.

Mount Bintumani is located in the North East of the country and rises to a height of 1,948 meters (6,381ft). The area has been designated a non-hunting forest reserve since 1952, which means it is pretty much teeming with wild life, including monkeys and exotic birds. Known as Loma Mansa ("the king of mountains") in Koranko it takes around 5 days walking through rain forest and bush to get up and down the mountain from Yiffin. Bintumani is the local name of the female spirit that is said to inhabit the mountain.

Our plan was to spend the first night in Yiffin, hopefully find a local guide who was willing to accompany us, then spend two to three days trekking the 30 miles or so to the peak of the mountain. We had taken enough supplies to last us for a week but were intending to rely on being able to find hospitable locals to accommodate us at night en route.

Arriving in Yiffin an hour or so before nightfall, we tracked down the head teacher of the local primary school, who generously offered to put us up for the night, and also found someone to guide us, at least for the first part of the trek. We also made a courtesy call on the local chief. Early the following morning we set off. Not far from Yiffin we encountered a remarkable bridge made from roots and lianas. The 'Hammock Bridge' had been built by the secret societies, who had used their magic to make it strong and ensure it wouldn't fall into the swelling river below.

The first night was spent sleeping on the hard and uneven mud floor of a grass hut but we were so tired that we slept solidly for eight hours until the morning sun woke us streaming through the wooden shutters which passed for windows. It rained quite heavily during the afternoon, but we soon dried off when the sun came out, and we spent a second night on the mud floor of a hut.

The morning we started the final ascent to the peak, climbing most of the time up gently sloping open grassland, our guide announced that that was as far as he was going. You could see the peak and it was pretty obvious which way to go, so we pressed on without a guide. The final stretch to the summit was pretty steep and we had to use the long tough grass to pull ourselves up whilst using rocks as footholds. Then we reached a wide plateau surrounded by stunning views in all directions and marked with a cairn of rocks. We had reached the summit!

Re-tracing our steps we made our way back towards Yiffin, acquiring a guide on the way. Two days later we arrived back at the head teacher's house where we had left the Land Rover for safe-keeping, and breathed a sigh of relief that it was in the same state as we had left it. We were exhausted, muddy, and (having worn the same pair of underpants for five days) I had acquired a painful version of dhobies itch, as well as a couple of blisters, but it gave us a great sense of achievement to have been where few other white people had trod and to have conquered the mountain.

A few weeks later I wrote to the Marvins, who had by now moved from Butimba Teachers' College in Tanzania to the civilisation and relative sophistication of Dakar in Senegal, where Ian was now the KELT adviser to the Senegalese-British Institute.

May 18th 1982
Makeni

Dear Ian, Manh and Khiao,

Greetings from down the coast! Dakar sounds very attractive after the rigours of life in Mwanza. I'm glad Manh is enjoying it. Is Khiao now fluent in French? Makeni is definitely an improvement on Tabora in Tanzania, but is rapidly going downhill. There are rumours that the sole supermarket is soon to close because the Lebanese trader who runs it can't make a big enough profit, in spite of employing people whose sole duty is to go round rubbing off the old prices and putting on a higher one. Even a tin of baked beans costs the equivalent of £1.50! But you *can* buy things like prawn crackers, tinned raspberries and John West salmon - the latter at £5 a tin - so things are not yet too bad! The worst news is that the brewery has shut down because it has no foreign exchange allocation to buy hops and whatever other ingredients you put it beer. But there is still a plentiful supply of fine French wines at not-too-ridiculous prices, and of course the ubiquitous local palm-wine, known as "from God to man".

I have a minute flat on the college campus. Its great advantage is that it has constant running water and a regular supply of electricity twice a day.

The job is proving quite interesting, at the moment teaching in the college for four days per week, thought this should reduce to two days per week next term, and running in service courses with the local inspectorate for the rest of the time. I have quite a large area to cover - two-thirds of the Northern Province, but we expect to get three VSO teacher supervisors next term for the three districts in the province.

At the moment I am in frightful hot water with the British Council in Freetown because during the Easter holidays I went off with a couple of colleagues to climb Mt Bintumani (at 6500 feet the highest mountain in Sierra Leone). We used the Council Land Rover to get within 30 miles or so of the mountain, as the roads were so awful the Beetle would never have made it closer than 60 miles away. They had sent round instructions that nobody was to travel away from their home base during the Easter holidays because of possible election violence. Nobody would ever have known, but unfortunately Kevin, the local VSO mechanic, went to Freetown and by chance bumped into the Council's Assistant Representative, who asked how I was getting on, and before he realised he was putting his foot in it had said, "Oh, he's gone to climb Mt Bintumani." Next question: "Oh, did he go in the Council's Land Rover?" Silence....

The latest development was a letter, rejecting my last mileage claim on the grounds that the mileage was too high, and accusing me of "irresponsibility, lack of integrity and lack of foresight". I wrote a suitably repentant and fawningly obsequious reply, but I fear I may have dashed any hopes I had of a permanent post with the Council's career service forever if this letter stays on file. I suspect I still haven't heard the last of it. I suppose the worst they could do would be to give me the sack, as they did to another KELT in Sierra Leone last year, so I'm now just keeping my fingers crossed that they will forget about it.

In fact, with hindsight, it was a pretty foolhardy escapade. The New York Times reported on 2nd May 1982, under the headline, "Sierra Leone Voids Some Election Returns":

"Authorities threw out election results in 8 of Sierra Leone's 66 constituencies today because of "serious irregularities" in voting to elect a new Parliament. In some areas the voting was accompanied by violence.

Complete returns are not expected for several days because of poor communications in this West African nation of 3.5 million people. Although officials refused to say what the irregularities were, there were many reports of fights at polling stations Saturday as supporters of rival candidates tried to remove or destroy opponents' ballot boxes. Residents here said at least 10 people were killed. Other unconfirmed reports said that as many as 50 people were killed in remote regions in fighting between supporters of rival candidates." [29]

Several Teachers College staff were roped in as Returning Officers and Election Supervisors in Bombali District. John Conteh, the Head of our English Department, was in charge of the elections on polling day in a village about 70 miles from Makeni. They opened the polls in the early morning, and the day passed uneventfully, with villagers from several miles around coming to cast their votes. This was done, not by putting an X on a ballot paper, but by the voter dropping a marble into the sealed box for the chosen candidate. Towards evening they closed the polls and adjourned to the bar next door for a Star beer. About half an hour later, a grey Land Rover drove up, so they handed over the ballot boxes and carried on drinking. An hour or so later another grey Land Rover appeared, this time with "Electoral Commission" painted on the door. "But we've already handed the ballot boxes over to your colleagues who came earlier", Mr Conteh explained.

It turned out that the first Land Rover belonged to one of the candidates, who was taking the opportunity to move marbles around between the boxes. Needless to say, the elections in that constituency were declared null and void.

There was also a rumour (probably apocryphal), that one of the candidates in Freetown had polled 30,000 votes, which just happened to be the number of his green Mercedes.

According to Wikipedia:

"Parliamentary elections were held in Sierra Leone on 1 May 1982. They were the first elections since the country had become a one-party state under the 1978 constitution, with the All People's Congress being the sole legal party. Following an amendment to the constitution in 1981, prior to the election, primaries were held to choose up to three candidates (all selected by the APC) to stand in each of the 85 constituencies. As a result, elections in 66 of the 85 constituencies were contested (13 of the 19 seats left uncontested were held by cabinet ministers). The elections were marred by violence in which up to 50 people died. The APC used the army to crush opposition SLPP supporters in what became known as the "Ndogboyosoi [bush devil] war". In addition to the 85 elected seats, the parliament consisted of 12 paramount chiefs elected through tribal councils and 7 MPs appointed by the President, Siaka Stevens." [30]

7 KURUBONLA

During the summer I spent a couple of months back on leave in Exmouth, starting off with the week-long "Dunford House" seminar near Midhurst in Sussex, which was a great opportunity to exchange ideas and experiences with other KELT lecturers who were now being employed by the British Council on an increasing number of projects around the world. The key role of teacher training in curriculum innovation was:

"the primary concern of the 1982 seminar, during which participants were asked to engage in complex simulation tasks or syndicate exercises, exploring the interface between the agendas and priorities of the host country or institution and those, on the one hand, of funding agencies such as the British Council and the ODA, and on the other, of the individuals involved in the day-today professional contact". [31]

Then, with batteries recharged, it was time to return to Makeni for my second year there. During the four years I had spent in Tanzania, as my salary was paid in sterling in the UK, each month I had to cash a cheque in the local bank to convert this into local currency. I had never contemplated changing money on the black market. On arriving in Makeni, once a month, I had regularly spent a couple of hours during free periods cashing my monthly cheque in the local Barclays Bank.

It never seemed to take less than an hour by the time you had stood in the queue, handed in the cheque, then waited for it to work its way around the bank until finally it had been approved by the manager and you were called over by the cashier and given a fist full of Leones.

This particular morning it seemed to be taking far longer than usual. After waiting for a couple of hours, I was beginning to get impatient, as I had a lesson back at the college due to start within the next hour. I approached the cashier and enquired about the progress of my cheque.

"Oh, the manager wants to see you."

I surmised there must be something wrong with the cheque. Maybe I had forgotten to sign it, or the cheque which I had cashed the previous month had bounced?

A few minutes later I was wheeled in to the Manager's office. He introduced himself as the new manager, and we went through the usual extended formalities of greeting each other. Then he said,

"Why are you cashing your cheque in the bank? I can give you a better rate!"

I was somewhat taken aback, but didn't have much option other than to agree that he, rather than the bank, could cash the cheque.

However, when I discovered that the rate the manager was offering was a kind of "mean rate" between the bank's official exchange rate and the rate being offered by the Lebanese shopkeeper over the road, I resolved that in future I would avoid Barclays Bank and cash my cheques with the Lebanese shopkeeper. This took only a couple of minutes, rather than a couple of hours, and you got around 10% more than the bank rate.

Around the start of term, the promised volunteers arrived in the country and went off to spend a month learning Krio. The majority were recruited and administered by Voluntary Service Overseas (VSO), which in those days recruited primarily from the UK, with a couple from Canadian University Service Overseas (CUSO). The volunteer in Kabala (Mike Foston) was a VSO, whilst in Bombali District there was a CUSO. Unfortunately she didn't take to life in Makeni and left after the first few months.

Shortly after Mike arrived, I arranged to pick him up in Kabala and to accompany him on a trip by Land Rover to Kurobonla, about 110 miles north-east of Kabala, close to the border with Guinea and to the north of Mt Bintumani. This was the place in the district furthest away from Kabala with a primary school, so it would give him a good idea of the extent of the area he was going to be covering. There was a road marked on the map, though nobody in Makeni seemed to know whether it actually existed or not, or what state it might be in. Anticipating the road might be hard going, we set off early in the morning.

Not a lot has changed in the ensuing four decades. The "Awoko" website, under the heading "MP cries for Govt Help to Kurubonla" reports:

"The Hon Lahai Marrah, yesterday pleaded with the Government ... for support to his people in Kurubonla which is about 110 miles from Kabala, during the on-going parliamentary debate on the 2016 budget. According to Hon Lahai Marrah, educational facilities should be extended to the rural communities where children are suffering to access education, citing a village in his constituency (Kurubonla) [where] pupils who intend to further their education to Senior Secondary school level will have to either travel to Kono which is about 10 to 15 miles or they go to Kabala which is the district headquarter town, 110 miles away from Kurubonla. This, he explained, is responsible for the high number of school dropouts, and increase in teenage pregnancy whilst most of the boys with little or no options divert to motor bike riding (Okada), maintaining that most of his constituents focus on doing business in Koidu Town, Kono District which is very nearer to them. Hon Marrah maintained that the road being constructed from Sandor Chiefdom in Kono to Kurubonla was one of the main reasons why the people in that area voted for President Ernest Bai Koroma, ... as Kurubonla was known to be the strong hold of the opposition Sierra Leone Peoples Party (SLPP). The Honourable disclosed that most people will use the Kono axis to access Kurubonla instead of going through Kabala town through which people spend days to reach and in most cases vehicles stuck along the road, even the motor bikes find it hard to dodge the rugged roads." [32]

The road, though un-tarred, was in a reasonably good condition for the first thirty miles or so as far as Falaba. Once an important fortress town on the slave routes across West Africa, Falaba was besieged for five months by Mandinka forces in 1884. When the inhabitants were almost starving to death, its chief Manga Sewa gathered his family together in Falaba's gunpowder magazine and lit a torch, simultaneously killing himself and breaching Falaba's walls. The town fell into decline after 1895 when the colonial administrative capital moved to Kabala. Beyond Falaba, the road gradually deteriorated until it became nothing more than a footpath, switching from side to side of what had once been the road, with bushes and small trees growing on either side of the path. At one point the Land Rover got stuck on a projecting rock and had to be pushed and pulled by some passing villagers until all four wheels made contact with the ground again. It was impossible to do more than 10 miles per hour, and it was almost dark by the time we finally reached Kurubonla. Having tracked down the Head Teacher's house, we introduced him to Mike and explained that he was their new district level teacher supervisor and would be visiting Kurobonla from time to time to run in-service workshops for English teachers from primary schools in the area around Kurobonla.

"Oh, we've heard that before", the Head Teacher exclaimed. "About five years ago, a Peace Corps teacher came and said the same thing, that he would be coming back and running workshops for the teachers, but we never saw him again!"

We assured the Head Teacher that this would definitely not be the case with their new volunteer! Then we were taken to visit the town Chief, where we given a warm welcome, sat on the veranda drinking palm wine and treated to a meal of rice with plasas, while the Head Teacher explained, in what I guessed to be Koranko, the purpose of our visit.

Having spent the night in the Head Teacher's house, we set off at crack of dawn for the long drive back to Kabala. Imagine our amazement when we found that for the first ten miles or so, the bushes, small trees and long grass obscuring the path had been chopped down during the night, and what had been a twisting and winding track was transformed into a 6 foot wide swathe of chopped grass, forming a passable road once again. I said to Mike, "Well, after all this effort, you really will have to make regular visits on your motorbike to Kurubonla!"

8 IN-SERVICE TRAINING WORKSHOPS

Some of my most pleasant memories of Sierra Leone are of the times I spent running in-service training workshops for the primary school teachers. Over the course of time we developed a package of workshops on a wide variety of topics, and on the days we were not teaching in the colleges we organised workshops and school visits with the teacher supervisors and VSOs in our districts. These had a dual aim - to induct the VSOs and teacher supervisors in the use of the workshop packages, as well as trying out new workshops, gaining useful feedback on the workshop content and monitoring the impact of the project on teachers in the primary schools.

Primary teachers were poorly paid at the best of times, and often their salaries were several months in arrears. Despite this they were generally enthusiastic and well-motivated and seemed to enjoy attending workshops together with other teachers from nearby schools.

I remember going to a small rural school along the road towards Kabala. Built of mud, with a rusty tin roof and only two classrooms, the school had only two teachers. One taught the lower primary classes and the other the upper primary groups. Total enrolment was around sixty. After observing some lessons taught by each of the teachers and providing them with what I hoped was useful feedback, I asked about one older-looking boy who had been sitting on his own at a single desk under a large and shady mango tree all morning.

"What's going on with that boy sitting under the mango tree? Is he being punished for doing something he shouldn't have?" I asked.

"Oh, no, he's Class 7", came the reply.

So we added teaching mixed ability groups to the growing list of workshop topics!

In the more remote rural areas, despite being informed well in advance by the local inspectorate office, the head teachers would not believe that a workshop was going to happen on the stated day and time until someone actually turned up in the village. So it was advisable to arrive at least the night before, and preferably a day earlier. The Head Teacher would then send out runners to the nearby primary schools, often up to 10 or 15 miles away, telling them to send their teachers for the start of the workshop at 0900 a.m. the next day. If the workshop was planned to take a couple of days, teachers from the other schools would stay in the village with the local teachers or with family and friends.

Usually the workshops lasted only for a morning, and were followed by a communal meal. The KELT project would normally contribute towards the cost of the food, and the school would provide palm wine and some soft drinks. Generally the food would be rice with chicken soup or plasas made from potato or cassava leaves, sometimes mixed with dried fish, but in the Northern Province especially, one of the greatest delicacies was monkey soup. This was heavily seasoned with chilli peppers and the guest of honour might be given the monkey's head or other choice parts. It was a bit disconcerting to see tiny hands and feet floating about in the soup cauldron. It was a great insult in Sierra Leone not to eat what was set before you, so you just had to pretend it was chicken or goat and swallow it down.

Once on the way to a workshop in Tonkolili district, a flock of about six or seven sheep ran across right in front of the Land Rover as I was speeding at 50 or 60 m.p.h. along the two-lane tarred super-highway towards Koidu. It was impossible to avoid hitting and killing one of them, and as we got out to survey the damage an angry villager appeared demanding compensation for the dead animal. The price he quoted seemed extremely high, but it was explained that the reason he was demanding such a high price was because the sheep was pregnant with six potential offspring. Quite how he knew there were six foetuses was a mystery, but it was a hard to take issue with this, so I dug deep into my wallet and paid up. However, having paid well over the odds, we insisted on taking the dead sheep with us and delivered it to the Head Teacher's house to be cooked for a post-workshop feast. The teachers were unanimous in declaring it was the best workshop they had ever attended!

One of the things I found remarkable in the bigger primary schools was that often there was just one very large room with earth walls and a tin roof, which was divided into smaller sections by grass matting. This meant that the entire school could hear everything being said in any of the classes. As a lot of the time the children in several different classes were chanting in chorus, reading as a whole class what the teacher had copied out onto the blackboard, or singing songs at the tops of their voices, I used to wonder how they managed to make out what their own class teacher was saying and how teachers distinguished individual pupils' answer or questions against the background cacophony. It was surprising how much learning did seem to be going on in spite of the din.

Often the primary teachers' own English left something to be desired. They often mixed up Krio and English, and sometimes taught things which were just plain wrong. I remember observing one class where the teacher was teaching a fairly traditional grammar lesson about the plurals of some common nouns. I was pleased to see that rather than telling the pupils everything, she was eliciting the information from them:

"Who can tell me what this is ?"

"A book," chorused the children.

"And what is the plural of book?"

"Books."

"Good. Now what is this? Abu?" (pointing to the table)

"A table, " Abu replied

"Very good. And the plural of table, everybody?"

"Tables, " chorused the pupils.

"Now a more difficult one." (drawing a house on the blackboard). What is this, Ali?"

"A house", Ali replied.

"And what is the plural of house? Aminata."

"Houses!" shouted a little girl from the back of the class.

"No, you are wrong. The plural of house is hice. Like mouse. Mouse - mice. House - hice."

9 TRANSFER TO FREETOWN

I had been based in Makeni for nearly two years when it was announced that the KELT lecturer based at Freetown Teachers College, who had originally been tipped to take over in due course from Anne Hayes as Project Leader, was not going to be extending his contract for a second two-year term. The Council then came up with the idea that I should move to Freetown and take over his pre-service duties at the Freetown Teachers College and in-service training.

A Maths lecturer, Pat Hughes, had recently been recruited and arrived to take up his post in Freetown, and the Council also had a newly arrived Assistant Representative, Malcolm Johnson, who had replaced Colin Stevenson.

It was one of Malcolm's tasks to find somewhere suitable for Pat Hughes to live in advance of his arrival. We later surmised that he had approached an estate agent, who realising he was not well versed in the ways of Sierra Leone, had steered him in the direction of a property which was proving impossible to let, telling him that there was nothing much else available, and convincing him sign a two-year lease for a not inconsiderable monthly rental.

The house was totally unsuitable. It was located on Pademba Road, directly opposite the main gate of the Pademba

Road Prison, and next door to a busy BP petrol station where there were long queues for petrol every day (and occasional fights over places in the queue), and even far into the night. The house had a gloomy dark wood panelled entrance hall, around seven bedrooms and various bathrooms - rumour had it that a one time it had previously been a brothel - and to cap it all, the kitchen window looked out directly onto a row of five latrines with no doors, and the shanty town beyond. Pat Hughes took one look at this place and refused point blank to move in, insisting that the Council should find him another place to live. He eventually found somewhere just off Spur Rd which was a much more desirable place to stay.

So, I was informed that, as the Council had leased the place for two years and would find it very hard to wriggle out of the lease without paying punitive costs, I, as a bachelor, would have to move in when I was transferred to Freetown at the start of the next college term.

Back in Makeni, Fanta had in the meantime moved in with me and we were staying together in the tiny flat owned by the college. I took her with me on my next trip to Freetown and we went to have a look at the house in Pademba Road together. Fanta took one look at the place and told me, "If you move here, you're moving in on your own." Not only was it far too big for just one or two people, its location right opposite the prison made it quite a dangerous place to live - if there was any rioting in Freetown, the road outside the prison was one of the most likely spots for trouble, given the large numbers of political prisoners locked up inside. And the view from the kitchen over the five latrines and shanty town beyond was the clincher.

I confronted Malcolm back in the office.

"I'm quite happy to move to Freetown but frankly I'm really not willing to move into this house."

"I'm afraid you don't have any option, as we've rented it for two years."

"O.k., I'll just find somewhere else myself and pay my own rent, until you can get out of the lease on Pademba Road."

It wasn't too difficult to find somewhere more congenial. I discovered a small two-bedroomed bungalow in a very good state of repair on the CFAO compound in King Tom, and within a few weeks CFAO had repainted the house, and I had signed the lease and moved in ready for the start of the next term. Eventually the Council paid three months' rent to get out of the lease they had signed on the house opposite the prison, and with some reluctance agreed to take over the rent payments on the CFAO bungalow.

The CFAO compound had well-maintained gardens full of lush tropical plants. King Tom was a peninsula, with a single access road from Kroo Town - and the compound was very secure. It took only about twenty minutes to get to the Teachers' College in Kissy, where I was teaching two and a half days per week. The only downside I recall was that, although electricity was rationed and the lights came on for only a few hours each day, it was well within earshot of the King Tom power station, and you could sit at night in the darkness listening to the roar of the generators just down the road, running for twenty four hours a day around the clock.

We solved the problem of erratic electricity supply by getting a small Honda generator which produced about 2,5 kva of power, enough to boil a kettle, do the ironing and light the place.

King Tom was also the site of one of two main bomehs (rubbish dumps) in Freetown, and the sea around the peninsula was very dirty with all the rubbish which had spread from the dump and found its way into the ocean.

Living in Freetown meant I came into closer and more frequent contact with the British Council and the Ministry. The Representative when I arrived in Sierra Leone was Mike Chadwick, who was on his final posting before retirement. Not long after my arrival, his calculator went missing in the British

Council office. Convinced it had been stolen by one of the staff, he demanded its return at all costs. The local staff held a meeting and decided to call in the "pot man", a traditional diviner who, amongst other things, was said to have the ability to identify thieves. The pot man duly turned up and began heating up his pot in a charcoal fire. The idea was that he would go round the assembled crowd in turn, and if you were the guilty one, the pot would stick to your stomach. If you were innocent, the pot would leave no marks and the pot man would move on to the next person.

However, before this any of this could happen, Mike Chadwick appeared to see what was going on. The pot man immediately turned on him and denounced him, "You are the guilty one". Suspecting he had been got at by the actual guilty party, whoever that might be, the Office Manager paid the pot man off and sent him away. No one thought much more about it until a few weeks later when Mike Chadwick was searching for an old file in a drawer he never normally looked in, and came across the calculator hidden in one of the files. Whether the guilty party had taken fright and hidden the calculator there, or whether Mike Chadwick himself had put it there and then forgotten where he had left it, nobody ever discovered.

On another occasion, Malcolm Johnson found that some foreign currency notes, including sterling, dollars and Yugoslavian dinars, had disappeared from his desk drawer, which was normally kept locked, but which he had inadvertently left unlocked. He threatened to stop all overtime, and various other perks and privileges for the local staff, unless his money was returned.

The staff decided amongst themselves that the best solution was to summon the pot man. This time when all the staff had been gathered together, the pot man was in the process of heating up the pot, when one of the messengers suddenly started to burst out in a hot sweat, with rivers of perspiration streaming down from his forehead. Finally he could take it no more and confessed that he was the one who had taken the money. When they went to the messenger's house, the dollars and pounds had already disappeared, but the dinars were discovered, hidden in a drawer.

Malcolm Johnson once showed me an amazing collection of "Nomolisia" which he had acquired. A Nomoli is a stone statue, usually carved from soapstone, but they can also be carved from ivory or granite. Some are quite small, five or six inches high, but the largest can be up to 11 or 12 inches. They vary in colour, from grey and brown to white, yellow or green. The figures are predominantly human, with very large forward pointing heads, broad noses, prominent eyes and full lips. Some of the figures are said to be extremely old, with some estimates dating them as far back as 17,000 BC. Once word got around that Malcolm was interested in collecting these figures, villagers would turn up on the doorstep, hoping to make a sale.

Various ancient traditions are associated with the Nomoli:

"The ancient inhabitants believed that angels had once lived in the Heavens. One day, as a punishment for causing bad behaviour, God turned the angels into humans and sent them to Earth. The Nomoli figures serve as representations of those figures, and as a reminder of how they were banished from the Heavens and sent to Earth to live as humans. Another legend dictates that the statues represent the former kings and chiefs of the Sierra Leone region, and that the local Temne people would perform ceremonies during which they would treat the figures as if they were the ancient leaders. The Temne were eventually displaced from the area when it was invaded by the Mende, and the traditions involving the Nomoli figures lost. While various legends may provide some insight into the origins and purposes of the figures, no single legend has been definitively identified as the source of the statues. Today, some local tribes in Sierra Leone view the statues as figures of good luck, intended as guardians. They place the statues in gardens and fields in hopes of having a bountiful harvest. In some cases, in times of bad harvest, the Nomoli statues are whipped ritualistically as punishment". [33]

As well as being regarded as rice gods bringing a good harvest, sometimes the figures are hidden in a hut or buried in the ground by childless couples anxious to have children.

Whilst the statues generally represent human beings, they can also look like lizards, elephants or monkeys. Usually the head is disproportionately large compared with the body. Others represent a large terrifying-looking adult accompanied by a small child. Whilst some researchers date them as thousands of years old, other estimates have put the figures at around 500 BC.

I sometimes wonder if we are too rational in the western world and if there are forces at work in society which we ignore at our peril. The power of mind over matter tends to be underestimated. For example, the placebo effect is a well-known phenomenon in medicine - if you believe a medicine is going to cure you, it might well do so, even if it has no medicinal properties; and if you have paid a high price for a drug, it is more likely to be effective than a cheap generic version of the same thing. Homeopathy is dismissed by most people nowadays as mumbo jumbo, but it may still be effective, due to the placebo effect.

A striking example of mind over matter took place one day when I was in the British Council office cutting some stencils for the Gestetner ink duplicator, using a "Gestefax" electronic stencil cutter. This had a circular drum, and you attached the original document to be copied at one end of the drum, then attached the stencil at the other end. You secured the stencil in place with two clips, then pressed the start button and the drum whizzed round for a couple of minutes at 300 or 600 revs per minute, cutting the stencil. This could then be used to print multiple copies using an ink duplicator, a somewhat messy process. The advent of the photocopier soon made ink duplicators redundant!

The Gestefax was flawless. It was the first scanner, pre-digital technology. It actually produced a stencil by burning a hole with an electric spark.

Fanta appeared at the door asking to be driven somewhere. Engrossed in what I was doing, I tried to put her off. "Just wait downstairs. I'll only be a few minutes, then I'll take you". She flew into an instant rage, "No, I need to go right now."

I dug my heels in, but could feel waves of hostility at my refusal to do what she wanted straight away. By now, she had stormed off in a huff, and I went back to stencil cutting. Having attached the next original and the stencil to the drum, I pressed the button. It started up and was about half-way through the cycle, when there was a loud bang and the drum stopped revolving. Both the clips on the stencil had broken at the same time! For one to break would be unfortunate, but for both to break at once did make me wonder about what might happen if I upset Fanta really badly another time!

There was a British Council messenger named Tommy Koroma, a very kind and helpful guy who was a real expert at working the Gestetner duplicator. Several years later he ended up getting married to Teresa Harvey, a career British Council officer who had climbed up through the ranks as a librarian and had recently taken over as the British Council Representative. Sadly Teresa passed away not long afterwards.

Petty theft was rife in Sierra Leone. We had a KELT stationery store in the British Council office, to which only I had the keys. At the start of the year I made an inventory, and each item had a card for signing out. Every time something was removed from the store, I was fastidious about recording this on the card. Yet when I did the stock check a year later, 100 reams of duplicating paper had gone missing. I could only assume someone else had a duplicate key I knew nothing about.

I remember the CUSO Director, David Shears, complaining that a large quantity of duplicating paper had gone missing from the CUSO office and turned up in a stationery store just down the road.

At Freetown Teachers College we had an old freezer in the staff room where the lecturers used to keep bottles of cold water and not much else. We arrived back one Monday after the weekend to find that someone had carted it off, despite there being several security guards around the place. Then later someone stole the college generator, so for a whole term until money could be found to buy a replacement, we had to finish classes half an hour early, once it got dark, or else carry on teaching the final lesson of the day by the light of a bush lamp!

There was also an incident when the Representative's secretary was caught in the small hours of the morning loading hundreds of envelopes into a vehicle parked outside the back door of the office. She was married to the office Accountant and was dismissed for gross misconduct. He resigned from the British Council shortly afterwards.

On one occasion I was running some in-service workshops together with Martin Seviour, the VSO based in Kambia, on the north-western border with Guinea. Accommodation had been arranged for me in a spare room in the head teachers house. I arrived quite late in the evening, after a long drive from Makeni, took my briefcase and bag with clean clothes out of the Land Rover, which was parked just outside the bedroom window, arranged my safari suit for the next morning over the back of a chair and left a wet towel to dry on the other, and after a substantial meal of rice and plasas washed down with a few Star beers, I retired to bed and tucked in the mosquito net. It was very hot so the wooden shutters which served as windows were left open to let a bit of air in, and I was wearing only a pair of boxer shorts.

I slept soundly until woken by the sunlight streaming in through the window as the sun rose over the horizon. Needing to visit the toilet, I looked around for the towel I had left over the back of the chair. No sign of it. Nor was there any sign of the safari suit or the other clothes I had left in a neat pile on the top of a chest of drawers.

Realisation slowly dawned. Grabbing the bedsheet from the bed, I wrapped it around me and stepped outside into the compound.

"I've been robbed," I announced to anyone who was listening.

The head teacher produced a pair of trousers and I went out to check on the Land Rover. The tank was almost empty - all the petrol had been siphoned out. But the thieves had taken pity on me. Neatly folded on the roof of the landrover was the top of one safari suit, and the (non-matching) trousers from another, plus a towel and a pair of underpants. The other safari suit top, trousers, some shirts, and various other items of clothing had all disappeared. The thieves must have fished the clothes out through the open window with a long pole. Apparently quite a common occurrence in Kambia.

Perhaps linked to this propensity for things to disappear was a reluctance to throw anything away. Most things got recycled or re-used in some way rather than finding their way to the rubbish dump.

There was a global scare about the dangers of asbestos dust in the early 80s. The British Council decided to do a survey of its global estate and to remove any asbestos found in the buildings. It turned out that the Council office on Tower Hill had an asbestos roof, so plans were made to vacate the entire building for two months whilst the contractors removed the asbestos and replaced it with a new roof. The office staff were temporarily relocated to a large unoccupied house belonging to the High Commission up at Hill Station.

I had to pass by the office one day to collect something from the stationery store. I noticed that the contractors had removed all the asbestos from the roof, but instead of lowering the sheets gently to the ground had just dropped them from a great height, where most had shattered into shards of broken asbestos. The British Council's gardener, bless his soul, had laboriously collected all these broken shards of asbestos and was in the process of using them to edge the borders of the garden!

10 BILHARZIA AND BEAUTIFUL BEACHES

Sierra Leone has some of the most beautiful, and most deserted, beaches in the world. One of the rewards of moving to Freetown was the chance to go regularly at weekends to the beaches along the peninsula to the east of Freetown. We often went on a Saturday or Sunday to Lakka beach, about half an hour's drive away, usually taking a charcoal stove and ample supplies of Star beer, then barbecuing prawns, meat and fish in between sunbathing and swimming. Sometimes we just spread out towels on the beach, but other times we rented a small beach hut made of grass and banana leaves for the day to keep off the hot sun. Often we had the whole beach to ourselves.

Nowadays there is a beach resort with ten bungalows at Lakka.

"Lakka Beach is ... easily accessible by road, yet it is completely free of the hustle and bustle that characterises the capital city of Sierra Leone. Lakka Beach resort is the perfect location for a family holiday. For those whose work brings them to Sierra Leone it provides a haven to recoup from their business pressures. If you are looking for a unique experience in a stunning location, then the Island is the perfect holiday destination for you. What could be more romantic than watching the sunrise over Africa and set over the Atlantic

Ocean. If this sounds like a holiday for you, give us a call and let us know when you want to come. The beers are on ice at the Island hotel bar and restaurant ready for your arrival!" [34]

Back in the early 80s, Lakka Beach was still completely uninhabited and unspoilt.

A few miles further down the coast was River Number Two, singled out by The Guardian in 2011 as the best beach in Africa:

"Some 16km out of Freetown's dust and noise is a piece of unexpected paradise. River Number Two beach, the location for the 70s Bounty ad, is a tranquil bay mostly frequented by NGO workers on their days off. With temperatures at around 29C, December and January are ideal months to go. Don't expect any frills, only beach chairs, parasols and a latrine in a shed. But there is a hut where they serve up huge prawn kebabs on spicy couscous. You won't be hassled by the beach sellers, but do buy one of their fresh coconuts to finish off your lunch." [35]

The British Council's Office Manager Muriel Stanley owned several round stone-built beach huts here and one hopes she finally managed to reap the benefits once tourism took off again after the civil war of the 90s.

But the piece de resistance of Sierra Leonean beaches was the beach at Sulima, in the far south-eastern corner of the country, close to the border with Liberia.

Fanta and I decided to spend a week there, accompanied by two of the VSO teachers, Mike Foston and Gillian Belben. We weighed up the odds on how best to get there and decided to risk going in the Volkswagen Beetle. There wasn't a lot of space for food and luggage so we travelled as lightly as we could, intending to find somewhere to stay once we arrived and to rely on buying food from local shops and markets en route. The route from Makeni took us via Bo and Gandorhun to Zimmi, and then southwards for the final 60 km, close to the border with Liberia, past the turn-off to the Mano River bridge which led to the border, then along a poorly maintained track, quite sandy in places but corrugated in others, for the final few miles to Sulima.

According to the Bradt Travel Guide, "Sulima really is the end of the road. It has the air of a place forsaken by Sierra Leone."[36] Sandwiched between the mouth of the Moa River and the Mano River (which forms the border with Liberia):

"this exposed wild misty coastline is a different country from the misty mountains and bathwater-warm seas of the Freetown Peninsula - here is only thunderous surf that only the foolhardy would want to swim in. Even 100m from the sea, behind the sandbank that protects the town, you can hear the roar of titanic waves battering the steep shoreline. It's a spellbinding place, nevertheless, with the best surfing in the country". [37]

There were no hotels, motels or guest houses, but we did find a large, square, well-constructed two-storey residence in a good state of repair just next to the beach, with two rows of huts, rather like stables, behind the house on the side furthest away from the beach. It appeared to be unoccupied, but eventually we tracked down a caretaker who informed us that it was a rest house belonging to President Siaka Stevens. We inquired if it might be possible to stay in the house for a few days. No, we were told, because the President might turn up unannounced by helicopter from Freetown at any moment. However, if we wished, we could occupy a couple of rooms in the huts at the back. Judging by the hundreds of empty tins of black Cherry Blossom boot polish piled up outside the shutters which served for windows, these rooms must have been where the Presidential Guard stayed when Siaka Stevens paid one of his infrequent visits.

The main occupation in Sulima was fishing, and every day the fishermen could be seen hauling their catches up the steeply shelving beach. Between them, they probably managed to catch a ton or more of fish each day. There was no electricity and no cold storage, so the only way to preserve the catch for long enough to get it to the markets of Freetown, Bo and Kenema was to smoke it. This was a major occupation for the womenfolk of the village and behind almost every hut there was a smoking room where the fires were kept stoked up day and night and from which the sweet smell of smoked mackerel wafted across the entire village.

From the village, a sand spit extended a couple of kilometres to the west, to the mouth of the Moa river, and six or seven kilometres eastwards towards the Mano River. The beach shelved so steeply that swimming in the sea looked extremely hazardous, but in the Mano River direction there was a calm lagoon which was ideal for swimming. The water seemed to be pretty clear, but quite salty and free of snails, so we decided there wasn't much risk of bilharzia, or snail fever, a tropical disease caused by parasitic worms living in stagnant or slow-moving fresh water, which can infect the urinary tract or intestines causing abdominal pain, diarrhoea, bloody stools, or blood in the urine and which, if left untreated, can lead to liver or kidney failure and even death.

I don't remember informing the British Council that we were planning a trip to Pujehun District. Had we done so, they would almost certainly have tried to dissuade us. Around Fairo on the road between Zimmi and the turnoff to the Mano River bridge we came across several recently burnt-out villages, but fortunately managed to avoid any direct confrontations. Only with hindsight did I realise that we could well have been putting our lives at risk, as in the aftermath of the April 1982 elections there had been an outbreak of serious violence in Pujehun District, especially in the Soro-Gbema chiefdom.

"The Ndogboyosoi War, also known as the Bush Devil War, was an episode of political violence that occurred in 1982 between supporters of the All People's Congress (APC) and the Sierra Leone People's Party (SLPP) ... The violence was centred in Pujehun District [and] was triggered by the ruling APC party's alleged electoral manipulation and the intervention of a special squad of customs police against supporters of the SLPP candidate. There was no process of reconciliation following the violence. Children of those killed in the fighting or of those who died in detention were among the first to join the Revolutionary United Front (RUF), a rebel group which began a civil war in eastern and southern Sierra Leone nine years later." [38]

Before leaving Sulima we stocked up with enough smoked fish to make plasas for several months. Some time later Fanta and I went on leave to the UK. I had had quite serious amoebic dysentery which had been successfully treated in Makeni, but I wanted to be quite sure I had shaken it off completely, so arranged for some tests at the Liverpool School of Tropical Medicine. Fanta had no symptoms, but we decided it might be a good idea if she also had a check-up.

My results came back. I didn't have amoebic dysentery, but I did have three different kinds of worm! Fanta, however, turned out to have contracted bilharzia - probably from the idyllic tropical lagoon behind the sand spit in Sulima. The doctor explained that the standard treatment was a drug containing antimony which was highly toxic and had to be taken in small doses over an extended period. But they were trialling a new single dose wonder drug which she could take as an alternative, although it hadn't yet been approved for general use in the U.K. They gave her two tablets, one to take in the morning and the other in the evening, and warned her not to drive as it could have side effects. Half an hour after taking the first tablet she starting shaking like a leaf, but after some time the side-effects subsided. When it was time to take the second tablet that evening, she said she wasn't going to take it because it was so awful. I tried to convince her that it was better to get cured now rather than risk liver failure in five years' time, and eventually persuaded her to swallow the tablet. This time, after a few minutes, she was violently sick. The next morning I phoned the hospital and explained that she had taken the first tablet and had some quite nasty side-effects but that she had vomited up the second one.

"Don't worry," the doctor said, "the first tablet was enough to kill anything, and the second was just to make quite sure. But if you're worried, do get her to come back and get re-tested in a year's time".

One place I found thoroughly fascinating was Bonthe Island. According to Wikipedia:

"Bonthe District comprises several islands and mainland of the Atlantic Ocean in the Southern Province of Sierra Leone. Its capital is the town of Mattru Jong and its largest city is Bonthe, on Sherbro Island. As of the 2015 census, the district had a population of 200,730. The district is the least populous in Sierra Leone. .... Bonthe district is primarily inhabited by the Sherbro people (who are the native people of the district); and the Mende people, who immigrated to the district from Mende-dominant areas in the southern part of Sierra Leone.

Bonthe District has one of the world's largest deposits of titanium ore (rutile) in the world. Sierra Rutile Limited, owned by a consortium of US and European investors, began commercial mining operations in Bonthe in early 1979. Due to poor mining policy, the region has little to show for this huge economic potential. There are no good roads, water supply or electricity. Bonthe District continues to suffer from one of the worst environmental degradation episodes in living memory.

The main economic activities include fishing, rice growing and palm oil plantations. Mattru is the main city, located 52 miles southwest of Bo, along the Jong River, which provides access to Sherbro Island and the Atlantic Ocean.

Bonthe district was first among the districts in the Southern Province to undertake voluntary resettlement of internally displaced persons (IDPs) in 1997 among all economic hardship and combatant activities. The District suffered a mass exodus of Internally Displaced Persons when Sierra Rutile Company (the largest foreign exchange earner, taxpayer and employer of mine workers) suffered damage and destruction when attacked by fighting forces in 1995, and during all phases of the war. The company terminated its operations. [38]

Back in the 80's, Sherbro Island was a calm and peaceful backwater, untouched by civilisation. Bonthe, the main town, had a population of around 8000, and could be reached only by boat from the end of the roads from Bo and Moyamba at Mattru Jong. The boat journey took a couple of hours passing mangrove swamps and rice plantations until the river widened out and dry land became just a thin line on the horizon . There was a VSO teacher supervisor based on the mainland, and it was part of my job to visit from time to time to provide encouragement and support. There were virtually no motor vehicles and only a few motor bikes on the island – it really was like stepping backwards in time. A century ago, Bonthe had been a thriving trading centre. As Thomas Aldridge observed in 1910:

"In the stores of the European firms, in the stores of the Creole traders and of the Syrians, outside the stores, on the roadside pitches, hawkers, pedlars, and itinerant hucksters all vie in their respective ways with one another. There is selling over the big counter, over the small counter, off the strap tray, out of calabashes carried on the heads of the little pickins [sic: children] and even from off the ground itself – all is trade, nothing that brings in 'cash monies' comes amiss." [40]

All that remains now are decaying and abandoned warehouses, with the names of once famous trading companies, such as CFAO and Paterson Zochonis (the makers of Cussons soap), broken seawalls and crumbling houses, schools, churches and mosques. One abandoned ship has a large tree growing up through its beached wreckage. The clock tower has lost its clock:

"American-style Krio board houses, brought back by returning slaves, stand next to long unused colonial water hydrants and the ruins of early European trading companies. An incongruous British telephone box overlooks rusting fishing boats on the seafront." [41]

My worst memory of Bonthe is of having been struck down by dysentery and having to squat in one corner of an abandoned building whilst pretending there was nothing the matter and I was just exploring the ruins

.

11 LIFE ONTHE HIGH COMMISSION COMPOUND

My replacement in Makeni was duly recruited. Mark, as I shall call him, was in his late thirties, married to Maria, whom he had met whilst teaching English in Zambia, and they had had the first of three small children, little Maria. I wondered how they would manage in one of the tiny flats at the college in Makeni. Mark was well-built with a full beard and looked a bit like the legendary absent-minded professor. He seemed to settle in happily, although on one occasion there was a huge row when his wife accused him of sleeping with another woman, grabbed the mattress off their double bed, dragged it down two flights of stairs, poured petrol over it and then set it on fire and left it to burn, with dire warnings of what he could expect to happen if he failed to mend his ways.

On another occasion, Mark informed the British Council in Freetown that his Land Rover had broken down irreparably. He had had it examined by a competent mechanic, who had confirmed that it needed a new gear box. I agreed to go with a British Council driver to tow the vehicle to Freetown so that it could be sent to the Land Rover agents for repair. On arriving in Makeni we found the Land Rover outside the block of flats, but there was no sign of Mark. We asked if anyone knew his whereabouts, but as they didn't, we got the keys off his wife, hitched up a tow rope between the two vehicles, with the Council driver in front and me in the one behind. I thought I'd just give the engine a quick try to see if there was any chance of getting it to Freetown without having to tow it. The engine started after a few attempts, but the gears wouldn't engage. I fiddled around with the second gear stick, which you use to engage four wheel drive. Suddenly the engine stalled. I tried again, put it into two-wheel drive, then into first gear and it went forward. Tried reverse, which worked fine. We unhitched the rope and drove around the college compound for a few minutes. There seemed to be nothing seriously wrong! However, we decided it would be best to drive it to Freetown and get it properly checked over, just in case. So much for the "competent mechanics" of Makeni!

As well as our basic salaries and various allowances, the British Council used to pay a cost of living allowance, or "COLA". This was based on a complicated formula and designed to compensate for having to buy what were seen as the essentials of the diplomatic life at grossly inflated prices in the local Lebanese shops. Twice a year someone in the High Commission would go around pricing items in the "shopping basket". They also took into account things like the security situation. You got the highest marks for lack of security if the embassy building had been burnt down or otherwise destroyed within the previous three years! For the previous year or so the COLA allowance had hovered around an additional £3000 per year. Then suddenly without warning towards the end of the summer term we got a letter from the Overseas Educational Appointments Department in London, explaining that due to changes in the local cost of living the allowance would be going up to £27,000 per year - far more than our basic salaries. Celebrations all round, but these were short-lived, as three weeks later a second letter arrived, enclosing a payslip which ran to three pages of incomprehensibly complex calculations, saying that following further changes in the cost of living the allowance had been reduced to zero, and that as a result I had been overpaid by £3000 and could I please send them a cheque to reimburse this amount. I disputed this and eventually they agreed that as the overpayment wasn't my fault, I could pay it back at £100 per month for the foreseeable future. Mark kept mum. It was only almost about nine months later that it transpired that OEAD had carried on paying him the allowance at the £27,000 p.a. rate, and only realised this when the next review took place. They had sent him a letter asking for immediate repayment of £17,000! Mark had replied that he wasn't in a position to refund the money as he had used it to pay off his mortgage.

A few weeks later I was back in the UK and called in at the pay section to clarify the arrangement for them to claw back my overpayment. In passing, I enquired what was happening with getting the money back from Mark. The clerk checked the shelf full of files and said,

"No, we haven't got anyone on the payroll named Mark."

"That's strange," I replied, "He was alive and well and living in Makeni just a few weeks ago when I left Freetown."

He went over to a filing cabinet and opened a drawer labelled "resigned".

"Ah, here it is. He must have resigned..."

History does not relate whether they recovered the money or not. Years later, I found out that there was a rule that if an overpayment had not been discovered within six months, you were not obliged to pay it back, but it seemed OEAD kept quiet about this at the time.

Around this time Anne Hayes fell head over heels in love with Femi Malamah-Thomas, who worked for the local Land Rover agent in some capacity. After a discreet whirlwind romance, they got married.

Anne applied for other posts and left Sierra Leone, and I got promoted from KELT Lecturer to "KELT Professional Coordinator". This meant I had overall responsibility for managing all the professional aspects of the project. Financial management, and performance management of the other KELTs, remained the responsibility of the Council's Assistant Representative. The lease on the bungalow in King Tom was due to expire, and Anne's departure meant that one of two bungalows occupied by British Council expatriate staff became available. The bungalow was located on the High Commission compound, just off a sharp bend in Spur Road, half-way down the hill from Hill Station heading towards Lumley Beach. The next door neighbours were the Asst Rep, Malcolm Johnson, and his second wife, Gordana, a blonde and athletic Croat whom Malcolm had met on an assignment to the former Yugoslavia. On the opposite side of the path to the main road was the other half of the compound, which included a block of flats occupied by lower grade expat staff at the High Commission, plus a tennis court and swimming pool. There was some extended discussion with the High Commission about whether it was appropriate for the bungalow to be let to a contract officer who was not a permanent member of the British Council's Overseas Career Service, and in the end it was decided that the lease could go ahead, but Fanta and I would not be allowed to make use of the facilities on the compound - the tennis court and swimming pool - except as guests of the High Commission or permanent British Council staff. Fanta felt quite strongly about this element of discrimination, but I wasn't too worried, as I was able to get round the restriction on using the tennis court by playing tennis with Gordana. Later I was to come across similar discriminatory practices in relation to teachers employed by British Council teaching centres who were not allowed to use Embassy facilities although British Council permanent staff could do so.

Then there was the occasion when Fanta ran out of some food item and went next door to see if she could borrow it from Gordana. There was a large chest freezer on the outside patio, and Gordana shouted to her to just go and help herself from the freezer. Lifting the lid, Fanta screamed and fled as if her life depended on it. It turned out Gordana had been trapping the numerous snakes which infested the compound and was keeping the frozen carcasses in the deep freeze.

A constant source of bother was large telegraph pole in one corner of the garden. There was a high demand for telephone lines in the Spur Road area, with not enough phone numbers to meet the demand. Every time we let a telephone engineer into the garden and up the pole, our phone used to stop working. We would then have to pay to get it turned on again. In the end we just refused to let anyone from the phone company into the compound, and after that the phone seemed to carry on working perfectly.

On one occasion, Fanta must have been away in Guinea and I went with George Reid, who by then had taken over as the Council's Representative, to a St George's Society dinner at the Cape Sierra Hotel. George too was on his own, as his wife Sheila was also away. We sat on our own to begin with, but as George knew one of the couples at the next table we pushed our tables together. At some point in the evening as the whisky started to talked, I launched out on a lengthy, graphic and rather rambling story about a naked Sierra Leonean lady who had jumped over the six foot high gate and taken refuge in the High Commission Compound at 3.00 a.m. in the morning just a few days earlier. I had been woken by shouting outside near the gate and grabbing a dressing gown had gone outside to check what was happening in time to see a naked girl, probably in her twenties, who appeared to have several cuts on her breasts and was stark naked apart from a pair of panties, leap over the six foot high gate and engage in animated conversation with our watchman, who then took her into his room and found a towel and gave it to her to wrap around herself, and went off looking for some water to bathe the cuts to her breasts.

At this point Malcolm appeared from the bungalow next door, clearly in a bit of a rage at having been rudely awakened from sleep, and insisted the watchmen threw her out of the compound back into the street.

I went back to bed, and next morning Malcolm summoned me, demanding to know what our watchman thought he was doing entertaining a naked woman in his room. The most I could get from the watchman was that he heard a commotion in the street, that apparently the lady lived in a house further down the hill, and her husband was in the habit of going off to the casino at Lumley Beach till the small hours, gambling. On this occasion he had lost all his money, arrived back unexpectedly early and found his wife in bed with another man. In a furious rage he had grabbed a kitchen knife and started attacking her, while she had dashed off and taken refuge in our compound, at which point Malcolm had shown up and insisted she be kicked out back into the street. Keen to get to the bottom of things and establish if the watchman was telling the truth, I drove down to the police station at Lumley and asked the policeman on duty if anyone had reported in the middle of the night that they had been attacked. "Yes, it's the last entry in the book", he answered. Sure enough, there was a note that a woman called baby had reported being attacked by her husband, had run away, taken refuge in the British High Commission compound, been asked to leave, and had then reported the matter.

At this point the gentleman sitting at the far end of the table opposite me said,

"Yes, that was my wife, but I've sent her back to Uganda."

I felt so embarrassed I wanted the ground to swallow me up, but he didn't seem too phased by my version of events and shortly afterwards I made my excuses and went off back home to bed.

12 PASSPORTS AND PAPERS

Some time before we moved to Freetown, I had some local leave due and asked Fanta, at fairly short notice, if she would like to accompany me on a short holiday to Senegal. The plan was to stay with the Marvins, whom I knew from Tanzania. Ian Marvin was now working at the British-Senegalese Institute. It turned out the Marvins would be away for most of the time we planned to be there, but they were happy to let us stay in their flat.

There was one minor problem - Fanta's Guinea passport had just run out. She contemplated taking a trip back to Conakry to get it renewed, but decided it would probably be quicker, easier, and quite possibly cheaper, to apply for a Sierra Leone passport. So she turned up one morning at the immigration department to enquire about the procedure for getting a passport. "You'll need three passport photos and $25", she was told. "Come back tomorrow, with your briefcase." She took this as meaning that some additional payment was likely to be needed to facilitate the transaction.

The next day she re-appeared at the Immigration Department, where she was told she would need a birth certificate, and was directed to an office on the first floor where a couple of officials were sitting at their desks.

It must have been pretty obvious that she wasn't born and bred in Sierra Leone, because when she said she had come for a birth certificate, the next question was, "Where would you like to be born?" As she had been living in Makeni for several years, she opted for being born there. Some leones changed hands, and a few days later she was the proud possessor of a Sierra Leone passport.

We had a great time in Dakar, dining in French restaurants, visiting the beaches and taking a boat trip to Goree Island, where the Maison des Esclaves is a museum dedicated to the memory of the hundreds of thousands of slaves who passed through the "Door of No Return" before being shipped off in appalling conditions to the plantations of the new world. The Marvins took us for a drive to Lake Retba, about an hour's drive away to the north, where there is an unusual lake with a very high salt content, and a vivid pink colour. Separated only by some sand dunes from the Atlantic Ocean, it is said to be as salty as the Dead Sea and it's very hard to sink in it. The pinkish tint is cause by bacteria which produce a red pigment in order to absorb the sunlight. Local villagers collect the salt from the bottom off the lake and transport it to the shore, where it is mainly used to preserve fish.

By the summer of 1983, we had known each other for 18 months and it seemed to be a good time to take Fanta to the U.K., introduce her to my family and give her an idea of what she might be letting herself in for. When we arrived at the immigration desk I sailed through the line for UK citizens, then stood waiting behind the rows of desks for non-citizens for Fanta to reach the front of the queue. The immigration officer gave her quite a grilling, which went on for about ten minutes.

"Why are you here?"

"For a holiday for six weeks".

"Where are you staying?"

"In Exmouth with my boyfriend's parents."

"Are you coming to get married?"

"No, I just told you. For a holiday."

"Are you sure you're not planning to get married."

"No, I have absolutely no intention of getting married."

"Well, where is your boyfriend?"

As I was standing right behind him, at this point I chipped in,

"I'm here, standing right behind you!"

This intervention seemed to do the trick as after a few more questions he stamped the passport and we were allowed to go.

My parents had decided that, as we weren't married, I should stay with them and Fanta should stay at my cousin's just down the road. In fact we had been living together under the same roof in Makeni and Freetown for nearly a year, but it seemed best for the sake of a quiet life to go along with what they had arranged.

We spend some time touring around the country, visiting Wales and then returned to Devon. One afternoon we were returning to Exmouth from Exeter and were stuck in a traffic jam. I said to Fanta,

"I suppose we ought to get married."

She said, "Are you proposing to me?"

"I suppose I am."

At this point she got quite stroppy, "This is not how you propose to somebody. If you were a Frenchman, you would give me a rose and you would go down on one knee."

"Well, I'm not French, I'm English."

"I don't care. It's not the right way to do it."

"Well, sorry. But you need to make your mind up."

I don't recall her saying yes there and then, but we did decide to get married, I bought her an engagement ring and we started making plans for the wedding. I would have quite liked to get married in Exmouth, but as this was going to be a mixed marriage with two cultures involved, we eventually decided that the best thing was to get married in Sierra Leone, on "neutral ground".

Some months later, after we had got married, we decided it was time to get a British passport for Fanta. I went along to the Consular Section of the High Commission in Freetown, where I was informed that, since the passing of the 1981 Nationality Act, the only way she could acquire British Citizenship was to live in the U.K. for three years (or was it five?). I was not at all happy about this, as in the normal course of events my job with the British Council was likely to keep me overseas, and we weren't likely to be spending anything like that long in the U.K. for the foreseeable future.

In fact, I almost got myself sacked, as just a few days after receiving this information, there was a Queen's Birthday reception at the British Council office where the beer and whisky was flowing freely. I drank far too much, virtually all the guests had left, and as I was staggering down the steps to leave the building I was apparently cursing and swearing about Margaret Thatcher, her government and immigration rules. Fortunately the only people who heard me were a couple of colleagues and the British Council Representative George Reid, who called me into his office the next day and gave me a thorough dressing down.

This was still a running sore, however. On Wednesdays there was a group of High Commission staff their friends who used to play poker and a few months later one poker evening after I'd had a few beers I was sounding off about the Nationality Act to the newly arrived Consul. He calmed me down by saying that there was a clause in the Nationality Act about spouses of diplomats not having to fulfil the residence requirement, and he would check up on the rules. The following week, he told me he had looked into it, and there was in fact a clause in the Nationality Act which said if you were a serving officer in the diplomatic service or the British Council and paid in the U.K., your spouse could become a British subject by naturalisation without the need to fulfil a residence requirement. So we filled in the forms and waited to see what happened. A few months later he showed me a telex which had just arrived from London, saying he should interview Mrs Woods and confirm whether she was suitable to become a British subject. He showed me his reply, "I have interviewed Mrs Woods several times over a gin and tonic at sundown and can confirm she would make an excellent British subject".

So, having by this time renewed her Guinea passport, Fanta ended up for a brief period with three passports, British, Guinean and Sierra Leonean. It was quite handy having a Guinea passport to enter Guinea and a Sierra Leonean passport for entering Sierra Leone. However, she was advised to get rid of the Sierra Leonean one, as if there was any trouble in the country, dual nationals of the UK and Sierra Leone were likely to be treated differently from those with only British citizenship in the event of, for example, needing to be evacuated due to civil unrest.

13 POLITICAL CHANGES IN GUINEA

Meanwhile in Guinea, major changes were afoot. Since independence in 1958, Ahmed Sékou Touré had ruled as the first President of Guinea. In 1960, he declared his Parti Démocratique de Guinée (PDG) the only legal party in the state, and from then on ruled as a virtual dictator. He was nominally re-elected to numerous seven year terms and succeeded in wiping out any opposition by imprisoning or exiling the strongest opposition leaders. It is estimated that 50,000 people were killed under his regime.

Sékou Touré was born in Faranah, in Mali - the same village as Fanta's father. This was situated on the bank of the Niger River. He was an aristocratic member of the Mandinka ethnic group and descended from Samory Touré, a Mandinka king who defeated numerous small African states with his large, professionally organized and equipped army and put up fierce resistance to Fench colonial rule until he was captured in 1891.

Sékou Touré went to a Koranic School in Faranah, then to a French-medium lower-primary school in Kankan. He was expelled from a Technical College in Conakry at the age of 15 for leading a student protest against the quality of food and soon, (like Siaka Stevens in Sierra Leone), became involved in labour union activity. During his youth, Touré studied the works of Karl Marx and Vladimir Lenin, among others. In the early 1940s he worked as a postal clerk in Conakry, and in 1945 founded the Post and Telecommunications Workers' Union (SPTT; the first trade union in French Guinea), becoming its General Secretary.

In 1952, he became the leader of the Guinean Democratic Party. His greatest success as a trade union leader was when workers across French Guinea went on a 71-day general strike to force the implementation of a new overseas labour code. In 1956, Touré was elected Guinea's deputy to the French national assembly and Mayor of Conakry, positions he used to criticize the French colonial regime. In September 1958, Guinea took part in a referendum on the new French constitution. French overseas territories had the option of choosing to continue their existing status, to move toward full integration into metropolitan France, or to acquire the status of an autonomous republic in a new quasi-federal French Community. If, however, they rejected the new constitution, they would become independent forthwith and would no longer receive French economic and financial aid or retain French technical and administrative officers.

Guinea was the only one of France's African colonies to vote for immediate independence rather than continued association with France. It became the only French colony to refuse to become part of the new Francophone African Community when it became independent in 1958. In 1960, Touré declared the PDG to be the only legal party and for the next 24 years, he effectively held all governing power in the nation.

When the French left Guinea, they adopted a "scorched earth" policy, knocking down bridges, ripping out telephone lines and destroying buildings at the airport in Conakry.

So for the next twenty four years, Guinea was run as a socialist state. Foreign companies were nationalised and economic plans centralized. Sékou Touré once stated, "Guinea prefers poverty in freedom to riches in slavery," and much of Guinea's mineral wealth remained unexploited and undeveloped. Between 1965 and 1975 he severed all relations with France, developing ties with the Soviet Union, Albania, Cuba and other socialist states. During this period, an estimated 1.5 million Guineans left the country and fled to neighbouring states such as Sierra Leone.

Guinea's main allies in the West Africa region were presidents Kwame Nkrumah of Ghana and Modibo Keita of Mali. After Nkrumah was overthrown in a 1966 coup, Sekou Touré offered him asylum in Guinea and gave him the honorary title of co-president. The Portuguese still ruled the neighbouring Portuguese colony of Guinea-Bissau and, together with Ghana, Guinea supported the All-African Peoples Revolutionary Party guerrillas in their fight against Portuguese colonialism. In 1970, the Portuguese launched an attack on Conakry in an attempt to rescue Portuguese prisoners of war, overthrow Touré's regime, and destroy PAIGC bases. The 350 men who invaded succeeded in rescuing the prisoners, but failed to dislodge Sékou Touré's regime.

Fanta was on her way home from school with some school friends when the Portuguese attacked Conakry, and remembers hiding for hours in a stinking storm drain when shooting broke out in the streets.

By 1982, Guinea's economy was close to collapse. Sékou Touré visited the United States and pushed for more American private investment in Guinea, claiming that the country had "fabulous economic potential" due to its mineral reserves. This was a pretty dramatic economic policy change that led him to seek Western investment in order to develop Guinea's huge mineral reserves. At this time, the annual average income of Guineans was $140, life expectancy was only 41 years, and the literacy rate was only 10%. Measures announced in 1983 brought further economic liberalization, including the delegation of produce marketing to private traders.

Sékou Touré suffered a heart attack while on a visit to Saudi Arabia in March 1984, and was rushed to hospital in the United States for emergency surgery, but died the following day.

Before a successor could be named, the armed forces seized power in a coup d'etat, denouncing the final years of Touré's rule as a bloody and ruthless dictatorship. The constitution was suspended, the National Assembly dissolved, and the PDG abolished. Colonel Lansana Conté, leader of the coup, became President, heading the Military Committee for National Recovery (Comité Militaire de Redressement National - CMRN), and around 1000 political prisoners were freed.

The following year, Conté took advantage of an alleged coup attempt to arrest and execute several of Sékou Touré's close associates, including Siaka Touré, former commander of Camp Boiro, where many thousands of political prisoners had been held during Sékou Touré's rule. [42]

Whilst Sékou Touré remained in power, Fanta had been reluctant to take me to visit Guinea. There was a deep suspicion of foreigners, and she felt it might not be very safe. With Sékou Touré gone, things changed, though not overnight. By the end of 1985, Britain announced it was following the lead of the U.S. and withdrawing from UNESCO. The New York Times reported:

"Britain, which 40 years ago was one of the key founders of Unesco, will withdraw from the 160-member organization at the end of this year, the Government told the House of Commons today. Timothy Raison, the Overseas Aid Minister, made the announcement, charging that the agency, the United Nations Educational, Scientific and Cultural Organization, is inefficient and badly managed and has been "harmfully politicized." It "has been used to attack those very values which it was designed to uphold, " he said.

Last December, the British served notice, as required by law, of their intention to withdraw from Unesco, complaining about what they viewed as an anti-Western stance. They also complained that Unesco spends 70 percent of its budget at its Paris headquarters, rather than in the field. But until today, the British had left open the possibility they would change their minds if Unesco made major changes." [43]

At the time of this announcement, the Minister for Overseas Aid implied that the funds involved, around £5 million p.a. would be spent on aid to Commonwealth countries, stating:

"The $9 million budgeted for next year's British contribution to Unesco will go instead to other educational and scientific activities, particularly in the Commonwealth." [44]

This was bad news for UNESCO but good news for Guinea, as shortly afterwards the government announced that, in fact, the bulk of the money saved would be spent in Francophone Africa. As Guinea had just moved towards a pro-Western stance, it was not surprising that, not long afterwards, it was announced that the British Council would be setting up a KELT project in Guinea. As there was no embassy or consulate in Conakry, the project was to be managed from Senegal.

All traces of the Guinea project seem to have disappeared - it is not mentioned in the list of KELT projects held in the Warwick ELT archive, [44] but by 1986 several KELT lecturers had been recruited including Peter Constable, Barry Watson and Jane Carey.

The project's finances must have been something of a nightmare. When it was first set up, the KELTs (who like us in Sierra Leone were paid in the UK) were told that everything should be done by the book, that they should change sterling in the bank, and submit receipts and make claims via the British Council in Dakar in the usual way. However, when one of the first items claimed for was a garden hose, which should have cost around £20 at the black market exchange rate, but at the official exchange rate came to £800, this advice was rapidly withdrawn and they were advised that funds would be sent in future via the diplomatic bag, to be changed at the best available rate.

Guinea had refused to join the Francophone African currency system in 1959 and introduced its own currency, the Guinea Franc. This was replaced by the Syli, which was used in the country from 1971-1985. Then a second Guinean franc replaced the Syli in 1985. The changeover in 1985 caused something of a crisis as the old currency was withdrawn, but the new banknotes were not issued until around three weeks later. So for several weeks there was no legal tender in the country and things reverted to a barter system.

Our first trip to Guinea took place over Christmas and New Year. We stayed in an unoccupied house courtesy of Fanta's brother-in-law, who worked for the Ministry of Education. On New Year's Eve we went out to celebrate at a local hotel, taking with us a large carpet bag crammed full with bundles of 100 Syli notes, tied up with elastic bands. At the entrance to the event were several tables where staff were counting notes (not each individual banknote, which would have taken forever, but just the bundles), before allowing people to enter.

The place we were staying was some distance from the centre of Conakry, beyond the airport. One night we were returning back quite late at night when we got stopped by armed police at a road block. I was driving, and Fanta was in the passenger seat. Without asking to see any papers, one of the them pushed his gun through the passenger side window:

"Get out of the car!"

"Why should I get out of the car?" Fanta replied

"Just do what he says," I whispered to her. "They might be drunk, or drugged, or trigger-happy. Anything might happen."

"No, I'm not getting out of the car." Turning to the policeman she said,

"Where's your superior officer - go and call him."

Somewhat reluctantly the policeman disappeared behind a hut and came back with his boss.

"Why do you employ illiterates like this?" Fanta ranted, "You take them from the bush, give them a uniform and make them stand in the road. Why didn't he ask for the papers? If he had asked, he would have seen that this car is my car and this man is my husband."

By now cowed into submission, the policeman motioned us to go.

"Take this woman away. Au revoir et bon voyage."

We went on our way. If you were a Guinean woman in a car with a European in 1985, the automatic assumption was that you were a lady of ill-repute.

It used to happy all the time in Conakry during this period. If Fanta was driving we hardly ever got stopped. If I was in the driving seat we would get stopped every few blocks and asked for our papers. Another time we were with Fanta's sister and I was driving. I had left my Sierra Leone licence behind and had only by British licence, which was a green sheet of A4 paper with no photo, which had been folded up to fit in my wallet but had fallen apart, so consisted of 16 small pieces held together by sellotape.

"This is not a licence."

"Yes, it is. It's a British licence."

"Pull over and get out."

It was clear that we were going to be at the side of the road for some time unless palms were crossed. We had only just arrived from Sierra Leone and had no Guinean currency yet. I fished around in my pocket and pulled out a 100 leone note, (worth around one dollar). There followed a lengthy debate amongst the policemen about how much it was worth. One said $100 dollars, the other said , "No, it's an insult. It's only worth a dollar."

Fortunately the first policeman was more persuasive and carried the day, so we drove off hastily before they discovered its true value.

14 PULLING OUT OF THE PROJECT

By mid-1985 most of the VSOs and CUSOs attached to the project had completed several years in Sierra Leone and it was time for them to move on. Whilst I was on leave during the summer, Brian, the CUSO who had originally been based in Koidu, but had been moved at his request to Magburaka, resigned at short notice and returned to Canada without finishing his contract, which was due to run until the end of the year.

He wrote:

" I don't imagine you were all that surprised. I had thought of staying for another three months with little to do apart from spend my American dollars. I don't suppose there will be much active work until nearly the end of September, and I've also heard that there may be elections in October, which will no doubt shut schools for some time.

I hope the programme is fine and that the books are being distributed in an orderly fashion. Excuses they may be, but towards the end of last term I started to notice considerable apathy from the teachers for the workshops. This may have been due to having no money and in some cases having to pay for fares and food when attending a workshop. Also the

Teacher Supervisor did not show great concern, except for the motorcycle. I think everybody was tired of hearing the same things repeated in workshops, and were beginning to wonder when they were actually going to see the books. As you well know teachers problems, you can imagine how much teaching was on their minds!

I made one mistake during my time there. I should never have moved from Koidu to Magburaka. I did not like the place at all. I know I wanted to, but I regretted it many times afterwards. The house was lovely, but the location was so far removed from the town. I had always thought I would like the privacy, but little did I know how much I enjoyed the company of the people who lived around me in Koidu. I missed my friends, the market, and the whole environment. I thought I would never say that I was lonely, but I surely missed Koidu. I would still be in Sierra Leone now if I had not moved. I thought of asking CUSO if I could move back, but thought how ridiculous I would be in asking for this after all the fuss of moving, so instead I decided to leave. I calculated there would be approximately six weeks real work left for me anyway. I do miss Koidu very much, even now, but that will pass.

I hope the motorbike has been retrieved from the CUSO rest house. The furniture I left in the house in Magburaka. The Assistant D.O. came to see me the night before I left and wanted to buy the stove. He said I could sell it to him, no matter if it was the government's property. I said no. He also wanted the keys to the house. I therefore left him the keys when I left, but Mr Gbendu was very upset when I told him, because he also wanted the keys. So I went back to the Assistant D.O. and asked him for the keys back and took them to Mr Gbendu. He was my Inspector of Schools, after all. Neither of the two men would talk to each other - I had previously asked them to reach some agreement amongst themselves.

Mr Bendu, the Supervisor of Schools in Magburaka, had me on the carpet when he learned that I was leaving. He wanted me to write a letter there and then recommending that George Halliwell, the Teacher Supervisor, should get the bike. I tried to tell him over and over again that it wasn't up to me, but he insisted. I refused, saying it was up to the KELT programme in Makeni and Freetown, meaning you and David. It did irritate me that all the programme was really worth to them was the bike and whatever they could skim from the books, cabinets etc.

Hope you had a fine summer Paul and Fanta, and that you enjoyed Greece. I hope you stocked up on gold, Fanta, to replace what you lost in Freetown. And I do not think it was me who left your fridge door open that last night I stayed in your house. If it was me, though, Fanta, please forgive me. I would hate to be over here and thinking you were still angry with me! Thanks for everything you did for me while I was in Sierra Leone. I appreciated it so much and you made my volunteer days so much easier.

Love, Brian".

Keeping the VSOs and CUSOs motivated was quite a challenge. As highly paid KELTs we could put up with the frustrations of life in Sierra Leone, slow progress with the arrival of new textbooks, and a monotonous died of rice, fish and potato leaves, but for the volunteers earning less than £100 a month there had to be a high degree of job satisfaction to keep them motivated.

I was able to pull together the lessons learned from the Sierra Leone Project in an article entitled "Pulling Out of a Project: Twelve Tips for Project Planners" which appeared in the ELT Journal in July 1988. [46]

In this article I considered some of the problems inherent in language teaching projects, particularly in the Third World, which relied heavily on external funding and expatriate personnel. Various strategies were suggested to help ensure that innovative ideas and approaches continued to develop well beyond the withdrawal of external human and financial resources. (See Appendix A).

15 A HOUSE FOR FANTA

Following the death of Sékou Touré, Guinea began a period of rapid development. For the previous twenty-five years it had been run rather like Albania used to be, with little or no contact with the western world. The main streets in the capital had a few multi-storey buildings sandwiched between mud huts with corrugated iron roofs. Our project in Sierra Leone was due to end by July 1986, but it looked as if there was an opportunity if we got our skates on to build a house in Conakry which could be let out to the expatriates who were beginning to flood into the country at a substantial rent. Then later on when Fanta I had ceased to roam around the world for the British Council, in my mind's eye I imagined an idyllic retirement spent in a beautiful purpose-built mansion with a balcony overlooking the sea, watching the sun go down below the horizon with a gin and tonic in one hand and a good book in the other.

Fanta began a search for a suitable site next to the sea on which to build, and I looked into the possibility of borrowing some money to finance the building project. Bank managers were very keen to lend money until they discovered where it was we wanted to build, when they rapidly took fright. But finally we persuaded the manager of Barclays Bank in Exmouth to let us re-mortgage the flat I had owned there prior to getting married, and use the proceeds to finance building a house in Guinea. That way the bank could not lose and if everything went pear-shaped in Guinea they could foreclose on the mortgage on the flat in Exmouth.

There were several false starts in trying to find a suitable plot of land next to the sea. Fanta did eventually find a plot and took me over to Conakry to see it. We were having a good look around when one of the neighbours approached here and asked,

"You're not thinking about buying this plot , are you? Not a good idea!" It turned out that the owner had already sold the plot twice to two different buyers and there was an on-going dispute about who it actually belonged to. We rapidly backed off and the search for a plot continued.

Finally, Fanta found what seemed to be the ideal building site - an empty plot next to the sea, in a village called Nongo which was just beyond the end of the tarred coastal road northwards, and still relatively undeveloped. Prolonged negotiations followed, with the owner and the chief of the village, and finally the plot was ours.

One of our friends, a British architect named Nigel Wakeham, who was working on IDA/World Bank school building projects in Sierra Leone and had designed a beautiful house for his own family off Spur Road in Freetown, was talked by Fanta into designing something for us in Conakry. The plans he produced were ideal for the site - the main living room and master bedroom were on the first floor, with a balcony overlooking the sea, and the other bedrooms, a breakfast room and kitchen were on the ground floor - in effect, an upside down design. The windows in the master bedroom were at floor level on both sides of the room, giving a through draught in hot weather and minimising the need for air conditioning. Fins projected outwards on both sides of the building - an idea commonly used in the design of school buildings in West Africa - and the roof projected outwards for several feet, thus keeping heavy rain from washing straight down the walls.

So, Fanta recruited some Guinean workmen, and work began on digging the foundations. There was a small two-roomed outbuilding already on the site.

We had some initial misgivings about the capabilities of the Guinean workmen when they managed to dig the foundations six feet away from where they should have been, which would have meant the garage overlapped with the existing outbuildings. Then at the second attempt, they managed to dig the foundations for the fins facing inwards rather than outwards. Finally, at the third attempt, the foundations were completed, heavy stones incorporated into the concrete footings, and concrete poured for the base of the ground floor.

Next they began to put up the walls for the ground floor. Nigel came over from Freetown to check on progress, but was horrified to find that the end walls were about six inches out of plumb.

"If you put another story on top of that wall, chances are it will fall down. They're going to have to pull the end wall down and start again," was Nigel's verdict. This was starting to get both time-wasting and expensive. Fanta decided the best solution was to get rid of the Guinean builders, who hadn't built anything to a high quality architectural standard for the previous twenty-five years, and to import a gang of workmen from Sierra Leone. Once this was agreed, the work seemed to proceed in a much more satisfactory fashion.

Although there was plenty of cement for making concrete blocks, there was an acute shortage of all the materials needed for plumbing, wiring, bathroom and kitchen materials, patio doors, floor tiles, decent roofing materials and so on. We did the maths, and decided it would be best to buy a container load of materials in the U.K. and ship everything to Guinea. We also ordered the green coloured roofing material from a firm called European Profiles in Ammanford.

Fanta was effectively the Clerk of Works. The builders couldn't be trusted not to steal sacks of cement, so someone had to stand over them counting things out, so she stayed in Guinea supervising the building whilst I continued managing the ELT project back in Sierra Leone. It had become clear that our house was not going to be completed by July 1986, and the school textbooks were only just beginning to arrive in the country for the primary project, so it was a relief when the British Council accepted my arguments for why we needed to extend the KELT project for a further year, to July 1987.

Most building projects seem to over-run their estimated costs, and this was no exception. By the time we had poured the concrete for the first floor and got the first floor walls up we were rapidly running short of funds. There wasn't much chance of me being able to borrow more money from the bank, but Fanta managed to come up with a creative solution by borrowing money from a Lebanese trader in Conakry, Mr Amir.

She wrote:

" The money situation is nothing to worry about. Mr Amir said I can borrow as much as I need, because he is confident that as soon as the house is finished I will be able to get someone to rent it straight away, without any problems. Then I can pay him back. So please, don't worry, the Lord is with us".

Mr Surr (pronounced "Saw") reminded me of "Happy Families", which we used to play as children, where one of the characters was Mr Saw the Carpenter. Mr Surr was the person Fanta trusted most to go and buy materials in Freetown which were either not available or were much more expensive in Guinea.

On one occasion Mr Surr had been despatched to Freetown to buy some tins of wood preservative for coat the beams used to support the roof. I arrived back from work one afternoon to find a runner had arrived bearing a note from Fanta in Guinea:

"I'm writing this in a hurry. Tried to phone you but the phones aren't working. Can you go urgently to the Guinea Embassy in Freetown and find out why Mr Surr has been arrested?"

It turned out that the Guinea police had arrested Mr Surr when he crossed the border and taken him to a police station in Conakry. Fanta had found out he was locked up and had been to see him, but he had no idea why he had been arrested. The Guinea police had taken away most of his belongings and he was being held in a tiny cell.

I attempted to find out what exactly was going on from the Guinea Embassy, but without success.

Meanwhile Fanta was taking food to Mr Surr every day. After about a week, they finally let him go, without any charges. It turned out to have all been a mistake. Someone whose surname began with the letter "S" had committed a crime in Freetown and escaped in the direction of the Guinea border, and the police in Sierra Leone had sent a message requesting the Guinea police to arrest him. Mr Surr had just been unfortunate in being the only Sierra Leonean whose surname began with "S" to cross the border that day.

At the beginning of January 1987, Fanta wrote to tell me that the container of building materials had arrived, just after I had returned to Freetown after spending the weekend in Guinea.

"I couldn't stop laughing when I read your letter about finishing the house quickly before the Lebanese mafia kills us. I could just imagine your face when something goes wrong. The container arrived on Saturday and after you left we had to get about another twenty signatures before we could get the container out of the port. By Thursday all the papers were more or less finished, and they said that by Friday without fail it would be released. So on Friday morning I was at the entrance to the port by 7.30 a.m. but it took a long time to get in. When I did finally manage to get in I saw the container with the number and everything correct on it, then the crane came and loaded it onto the lorry. We approached the gate for the final check when the guard said to us we couldn't go yet because all the papers were not signed. We went to look for the man who had to sign the papers, but he was nowhere to be seen, so we just had to sit and wait until about 3.30 p.m. By the time we had got all the signatures and returned to the container, they had already offloaded it, because any container that hasn't got out by 3.00 p.m. has to wait until the next day. So on the Saturday morning we went there by 8.00 a.m. and loaded the container again. This time we managed to take it out, and took everything to Jane and Laurence's except the water tank and the garage door, which they took straight to the building site. You'll be relieved to know that everything was o.k., nothing broken at all apart from some louvre glass for the windows which can easily be replaced here.

We checked everything and it all seems to be there, except for the heavy duty lock which we haven't seen yet, which wasn't in the numbered box. The patio doors were well-packed and there isn't even a scratch on them, the same with the baths and all the other things - I think we should say, "Thank the Lord". The company will not let me keep the container even for a day, so we were obliged to leave everything at Laurence's.

The electrician started work today and when he goes back, Mr Surr will come with the plumber. All the electric poles have been put up, and tomorrow we are fixing the garage door. The plastering is going so-so. Jane and Laurence have been really helpful to me, feeding and looking after me. And the day I got the container out Laurence was really helpful. I would never have managed on my own as it needed two people to make sure nothing got stolen - but he was there to keep an eye on everything."

16 A SHOT IN THE ARM FOR LITERATURE

Nearly all our efforts with the KELT project had been focused on what was needed for teaching English language in the primary schools, and as a result we had, at least to some extent, neglected the teaching of "literature." One could argue that what was needed at primary level was sets of simplified readers. But what about the language improvement needs of the college students during their two- and three-year training courses? Surely there was a need for at least some literature component to help develop the trainee teachers' own language skills and widen their understanding?

In an effort to meet this need, a seminar on teaching literature in the colleges was organised in March 1986. The main outcome was a draft syllabus for teaching the literature component of language arts in the colleges at both Teachers' Certificate and Higher Teachers' Certificate levels. This was then further refined in a series of one-day seminars in each college and at a review workshop in December 1986.

As I wrote in the preamble to the report:

"The present seminars were organised by the National Curriculum Development Centre of the Institute of Education, in collaboration with the British Council and the English Department of Njala University College. Participants included

105

nearly every member of the Language Arts departments from all five primary level teachers' colleges, selected secondary school teachers, members of the Primary Inspectorate staff, Institute of Education and Ministry of Education officials, and others interested in the teaching of Literature at primary and college levels." [47]

The seminar report included a ditty spotted on an office wall at the Institute of Education which summed up the challenges facing the teachers:

We the Willing
Led by the Unknowing
Are doing the Impossible
For the Ungrateful
We have done so much
For so long
With so little
We are now qualified
To do Anything
With Nothing.

We were fortunate to secure the services of a UK consultant, H. L. B. Moody, who had an excellent knowledge of the educational system in Sierra Leone, having worked as Curriculum Adviser for English in the early 70s and subsequently visited on two occasions. He was probably best known for his "Teachers Guide to African Literature", which contained summaries of many of the classics of African Literature in the Heinemann African Writers series, and he had also written a handbook on The Teaching of Literature in Longman's Handbooks for Language Teachers series. Now retired, he and his wife had renovated an old barn near Settle in the Yorkshire Pennines and he spent his time writing and tending to a few sheep and goats. Given that he was now in his seventies, I was a bit apprehensive about how well he would stand up to being rattled around Sierra Leone in a Land Rover for three weeks, but he seemed to be in his element. The travelling roadshow also included Mrs Philomena Kamara, from the Institute of Education, Mr John Karimu who had been lined up as my successor as ELT Project Coordinator, Florence Stratton and Julius Spencer from Njala, and the KELT lecturers from each college.

In each venue, Mrs Kamara outlined the "thematic approach" to teaching literature which formed the basis for the new syllabus. Mr Moody outlined a basic method of studying literature through a process of "guided discovery", and there were sessions on the selection and management of "children's literature". Other topics explored included "unseens", the intensive study of prose texts, creative writing and extensive reading. Participants were especially keen on the session on traditional/oral literature which explored how to make use of traditional stories, riddles, proverbs, songs and rhymes. The seminar report noted that Salia Koroma's song/poem "Riches in the Bush" generated a lot of lively discussion amongst the participants. Other sessions dealt with teaching and dramatizing short stories, using stories from the set book, "African Short Stories", and the teaching of language through literature.

Comments from the participants mentioned in the report included:

"It has been a wonderful seminar. We met with other people with whom we shared our various experiences and we were able to learn a lot from them."

"I appreciated the concept of the teacher as an organiser of the learning situation and not as a dispenser of knowledge."

"Similar seminars should be held twice a year."

"Although I am not an English major, I can even teach literature with much confidence now."

"When is the next seminar going to be?"

In his closing speech the Chief Education Officer, Dr J S Lenga-Kroma said, "Looking at the timetable of this workshop, the Ministry is assured that in the near future English the master key will have most if not all of its present faults corrected and our pupils will have a field day of success in all their examinations." [48]

17 LEAVING SIERRA LEONE AND ITS AFTERMATH

Time flew by, the work on finishing off the house was pretty much completed, and I was busy trying to tie up all the loose ends of the KELT project before it was handed over to the Ministry.

I went over one weekend and we spent a couple of nights camping out in the house before it was rented out. I remember the crashing of the breakers as we were dropping off to sleep and smell of fresh paint. It seemed a pity to have spent so much time and effort building the place only for someone else to have the pleasure of living in it. But we were about to move back to the UK, where I had secured a post with the British Council's Overseas Career Service, and we could be posted to anywhere in the world in six months' time. So we were anxious to get the place rented out, both in order to repay Mr Amir and so as not have to worry about it from a distance.

Back in Freetown I was looking for a buyer for the Beetle, and selling off unwanted items, while Fanta was in Conakry looking for a suitable tenant who could afford to pay at least twelve months' rent in advance.

She drove up late one afternoon in a taxi.

"What have you done with the car?" I enquired.

"It's a long story. Let's get a cup of tea and I'll tell you what happened.

The car had been mis-firing so the previous day she had taken it to the mechanic, who had cleaned out the carburettor and replaced the spark plugs and assured her that the car was in perfect working order.

She drove to the border, crossed into Sierra Leone, and was driving along a straight stretch of road when the car behind her began sounding its horn. Assuming the driver wanted to overtake, she slowed down a bit and left room for him to pass. But instead of passing, he just kept of hooting more and more insistently.

Then looking through the rear window, she saw flames shooting up out of the engine compartment. Screeching to a halt at the side of the road, she rescued her baggage and perhaps unwisely leaned behind the rear seat to pull out the two 20 litre jerry cans of petrol which were in the luggage compartment over the engine. Not having a fire extinguisher or any means of putting out the flames, she sat at the side of the road and watch the car burn. Then she flagged down a passing vehicle and got a lift as far as Freetown.

The following day we went back with a mechanic to inspect the damage. The car looked pretty much a write-off. What must have happened is that the Guinean mechanic had removed the petrol pipe from where it went into the carburettor but failed to secure the pipe properly when he replaced it. The force of the petrol pump had then caused the pipe to come loose and with petrol leaking out all over the hot engine the car had caught fire.

We arranged for the wrecked car to be towed back to Freetown and informed the insurance company. I think when they found out that we were leaving the country in three weeks' time they may have suspected we had just torched the car rather than having to sell it, but it seems this kind of accident was not uncommon with VW Beetles so they paid out as a total loss, which saved us having to sell the car. They also allowed us to sell the wreckage for scrap for what we could get for it. I would not have been surprised if the mechanic who bought it did not manage to get it back on the road again a few weeks later.

That was the bad news. The good news was that she had managed to rent the house for the next couple of years to Aeroports de Paris who had the contract for rebuilding the Conakry airport, and they were going to pay the rent in advance. So within 4-5 years the house would pay for itself, and we could move on without having to worry about it.

Time passed. After three months living in Watford and working in London on the Technical Cooperation Training Department's China desk, learning how to shuffle files around, the British Council posted me to The Philippines as the Assistant Representative for the next four years, then in 1991 we moved directly from The Philippines to Brazil. Apart from Fanta visiting Guinea for several months whilst we were in Manila, for most of the time the house was left to look after itself, with the tenants responsible for any minor repairs. I remember one minor crisis when the copper power lines supplying electricity from the mains got stolen and had to be replaced.

We were getting $2500 a month in rent, which was good money in the late 80s/early 90s. The first lot of tenants moved out and the house was rented out again, this time to Shell. But then disaster struck. By the mid-90s, lots of Guineans had built nice houses. We had something of an advantage with a house next to the sea, but quite a lot of prospective tenants were put off by the upside down design, with bedrooms on the ground floor. There was a glut of housing to rent. The market was saturated, and rents fell dramatically. You were lucky if you got $600 per month, rather than the $2500 per month we had enjoyed initially.

Then in 1994 I was posted from Brazil back to work as a consultant in Language and Development for the British Council in Manchester. By then we had two children, Marie the youngest having been born not long before we left Brazil. This meant we had to get by on my income alone, which was a lot less in the UK than it had been overseas.

We agreed the sensible thing to do was sell the house in Guinea, as the $600 a month we were getting in rent was hardly sufficient to keep the place in good repair.

All would have been well, except that the person Fanta agreed to sell the house to was Henriette Conte, the first wife of the President, Lansana Conteh. They agreed on what seemed to be a fair price, and Henriette Conteh gave Fanta $20,000 to get all the papers in order to arrange for the ownership to be transferred to her nominee. (She didn't want people to know she was going around buying up property all round Conakry). Fanta used the money to pay off the various people in the Ministry of Housing and elsewhere who all took their cut. It took two months to sort out all the documentation, then the time came to sign the papers and hand over the keys.

At this point, the President's wife threw a spanner in the works, saying she didn't think it was worth what Fanta was asking and she was only willing to pay 50% of the price they had agreed. Fanta was furious, and told her that, if she wasn't prepared to pay the agreed price, then the deal was off.

With hindsight it would have been wise to scrape together the money to refund her $20,000, but as all the money had been spent we didn't have the where-with-all to do that, and anyway the money had been spent in good faith. So that was where things rested. We kept the deeds to the house, and Henriette Conte backed off.

Nothing happened till around 2004/5. We rented out the house to a missionary family for a peppercorn rent, reconciled to the fact that at some future date we might have to spend quite a lot on upgrading it. Then the tenants left, and for several months the house was unoccupied, with just a watchman staying in the cook's quarters to keep an eye on it.

18 HENRIETTE CONTE GRABS THE HOUSE

In the middle of the night in early 2004 a band of Presidential Guards (the notorious "Red Berets") surrounded our house, kicked out the watchman, and took possession of it. Henriette Conte argued that because she had paid us $20,000 nearly a decade earlier, the house belonged to her. As she was the President's wife, there wasn't a lot anyone could do about it.

We tried to find a good lawyer. They were all very keen to take on the case until they found out who it was against, when they wouldn't touch it with a bargepole. Eventually we managed to track down a lawyer with a reputation for taking on the presidency and winning, who agreed to act on Fanta's behalf on a no win no fee basis. The case dragged on and on. Each time it came up in court, it was adjourned for some reason or other.

This went on for several years. By this time we had spent two years in Kathmandu, Nepal, where I was the Council's Regional Change Programme Manager, and then moved to Botswana where I was responsible for English Teaching in Africa South of the Sahara. Then out of the blue we heard that the case was being resolved and Fanta needed to go urgently to Guinea. We got the house back, but the Presidential Guards who had been living in it for the previous four years had totally wrecked the place. There were broken windows, doors torn off their hinges, smashed toilets and sinks, tiles ripped up - it was as if there had been squatters living there for several years, using the place like a cross between a barracks and a brothel.

Fanta got a Quantity Surveyor to estimate the costs of putting everything to rights and it was going to come to around US$ 350,000. We didn't have that kind of money, and it would have been crazy to try to borrow it given there was uncertainty over Guinea's future, with Lansana Conte, although still the President, becoming increasingly gaga,and his wife using her position to abuse power.

According to Wikipedia:

"On 19 January 2005, shots were reportedly fired at [Lansana Conte's] motorcade on its way into Conakry in what was apparently a failed assassination attempt. One bodyguard was reportedly wounded. Conté, who was unharmed, went on state radio and television that night to say that he had survived because God had not yet decided it was his time to die. He also mentioned "threats from those who do not wish to see the development of Guinea or those who obey orders given to them from abroad" and vowed that he would "not be manipulated". On the next morning, he made a public appearance to pray. In April 2006 he was flown to Morocco for medical treatment. Most people expected he would not return, but he did. Then in May 2006 riots in Conakry over the price of rice and fuel led to around twenty deaths as security forces savagely repressed the popular uprising. In August 2006 he was again flown to Switzerland for medical treatment. This time no crowds met him on his return to Guinea. Meanwhile, Henriette Conté, the President's first wife, was accused of flouting the rule of law and taking advantage of the President's physical and mental incapacity to abuse her power. In August 2006 Human Rights Watch produced a 30-page report condemning human rights abuses in Guinea, highlighting the power vacuum resulting from the President's on-going illness, and expressing concern about the future".

We contacted Human Rights Watch's representative in West Africa, Corinne Dufka, who ran HRW's field office in Dakar, Senegal from 2005-2011, but although she seemed sympathetic there was not a lot she could do.

Wikipedia continues:

"In an interview with journalists reported by Guinéenews in October 2006, Lansana Conté said that he intended to stay as President until 2010, which was the end of his seven-year term. Conté also said that he was looking for a replacement who "loves the country and will protect it against its enemies." In November 2006 Transparency International updated its annual corruption index. Guinea under Lansana Conté was then second equal as the most corrupt country in the world (pride of place for corruption going to Haiti). This was a matter of concern for foreign firms intending to invest in Guinea (for example to exploit its extensive bauxite reserves) as they were unable to operate in Guinea without paying huge bribes to highly placed government officials, but if caught doing so they could face legal action in their country of origin.

In the early hours of 23 December 2008, Aboubacar Somparé, the President of the National Assembly, announced on television that Conté had died at 6:45 pm local time on 22 December "after a long illness", without specifying the cause of death. Six hours after Somparé announced Conté's death, a statement was read on television announcing a coup d'état. This statement, read by Captain Moussa Dadis Camara on behalf of a group called the National Council for Democracy and Development (CNDD), said that "the government and the institutions of the Republic have been dissolved". The statement also announced the suspension of the constitution as well as political and union activity. " [49]

In the meantime we took the decision to sell the house, in its wrecked state, for what we could get. Fanta managed to find a buyer who was prepared to pay a modest amount for the house and the land, then spend a great deal on doing the place up. Fanta then took Henriette Conte to court a second time to sue her for the damage she had done.

We nearly lost the proceeds from the sale. We were by now in Botswana, and Fanta arrived at the airport with around $150,000 in $100 bills in her handbag. It had been a long flight from Guinea and she did not notice the ten foot high sign outside the customs hall saying that any amounts over $10,000 had to be declared. Nobody asked what was in her handbag, and a couple of days later I went to pay the money into Barclays Bank. The cashier said to me,

"Where's your paper from the airport?"

"What paper?" I asked.

"The one they stamp to say you declared the money on arrival."

"I don't think she got any paper."

"Well, you'll have to go back to the airport and get one otherwise we can't accept the deposit in the bank."

With some misgivings we drove to the airport and spoke to a customs officer. He marched Fanta out through departures, onto the tarmac, then back in through arrivals and stood her in front of the ten foot high sign.

"Didn't you read this when you arrived from Guinea?"

She explained that she had had a very long flight and hadn't realised she should have declared the money.

"Come over to the office."

At that point I thought, this is where he holds out his hand and asks for ten per cent. But no, he signed and stamped the form, gave it back to her and said,

"Next time, make sure you declare anything over $10.000!"

I tried to give him a few dollars as a tip, but he refused, saying he wasn't allowed to accept it. Anywhere else in Africa we would have been stung. My faith in the honesty and uprightness of the Batswana was confirmed.

Back in Guinea, Fanta paid regular visits to Dadis Camara's office trying to get the case for compensation moved forward. His brief period in office was scarred by a massacre in the main football stadium in Conakry.

Wikipedia reports:

"On 28 September 2009, opposition party members demonstrated in the Stade du 28 Septembre in Conakry, demanding that Camara step down. Although many branches of security forces were involved, the presidential guard "Red Berets", led by Abubakar "Toumba" Diakite, were responsible for the violence, firing on, knifing, bayonetting, and gang-raping the fleeing civilians, killing at least 157 people (U.N) and injuring at least 1,200 not just in the stadium but as many fled on streets. In response to criticism from international human rights organisations, the government said that only 56 people died and most were trampled by fleeing protesters. Following the event, cell phone photos from anonymous sources circulated on the Internet, showing what appeared to be many women being raped by Camara's soldiers. Few women spoke up about the attacks against them because of a societal stigma against the victims of sexual assault. However, Doctors Without Borders confirmed that they had treated several rape and sexual violence victims of the incident. For a people already accustomed to violence, the rapes were nonetheless especially shocking as they took place in the open space, under broad daylight, and were horrifically violent and often mortal. According to numerous witness accounts, women were horrendously gang-raped using gun barrels and other objects. Some were raped then shot with the rifle barrel in their vaginas." [50]

Then on 3 December 2009, Camara was shot in the head by men under the command of his aide-de-camp, Abubakar "Toumba" Diakite. Camara's bodyguard and driver were killed in the attack. In January 2010 Camara was flown to Burkina Faso. Elections were to be held within six months and it was agreed that the military would not contest the forthcoming elections. Camara would not return to Guinea and would continue his convalescence elsewhere.

Around this time the courts found in Fanta's favour and awarded her damages against Henriette Conte. But unfortunately she was unable to travel to Guinea to sign the papers as she had serious health issues. The money sat in the Ministry of Justice account for some time before being returned to the Treasury. Two and a half years later, when Fanta was well enough to travel to Guinea to collect the money, it turned out that someone in the Treasury, noticing that no one had claimed the funds, had helped himself to them and bought a brand-new 4 x 4 vehicle. What should have been in the order of $200,000 had dwindled to less than $20,000.

A new President is now in power, Alpha Conde.

So far, all attempts to get him to sign the papers authorising the handover of the money owed to Fanta have proved futile.

APPENDIX

Pulling Out of a Project: Twelve Tips for Project Planners
First published in ELT Journal Volume 42/3 July 1988 Oxford,
OUP.

The design of ELT projects

Many language teaching "experts", particularly in the less
developed countries, now operate as part of a project team
rather than working in the isolated singleton posts which were
characteristic of most external aid to ELT in the developing
world in the 1960s and early 1970s. A great deal of thought has
been given to the design and implementation of projects. The
characteristics of a project, including clearly specified aims and
objectives and a limited life-span have been delineated
(Mountford 1981) and numerous case studies in project design
have been documented (See for instance, ELD/CIS, The British
Council, 1980; Brumfit (ed.) 1983). The design and
implementation of ELT projects, particularly in teacher
education, has been the subject of several in-house seminars for
educators and teacher trainers organised by the British
Council (for example, Coffey (ed.) 1983). There is general
agreement on the need for detailed initial planning at the start
of a project, formative evaluation allowing for changes of
emphasis during implementation, and a final summative
evaluation towards the formal conclusion of a project.

Maintenance of projects

However, it seems to me that until recently not a great deal of
thought has been given to maintenance after the formal end of
a project, once the foreign so-called 'experts' have left and only

local resources, human and financial, remain. In a discussion of projects of a slightly different kind, Mike Beaumont has pointed out that the development of wind pumps and similar items of intermediate technology entails the following steps: research - design - manufacture - installation - maintenance. I believe that ELT projects often include the first four steps, but make little or no provision for long-term maintenance.

Throughout the third world one cannot travel far without spotting some rusting relics, the tangible remains of failed agricultural or industrial projects. The projects may have failed for a variety of reasons: inappropriacy, maladministration, over-dependence on hi-tech equipment, lack of spare parts for machinery, to name but a few. There is a danger that, unless we pay far more attention to the aspects of long-term maintenance, our language-teaching projects will similarly fall into disuse - though with fewer obvious visible reminders left as blots on the landscape.

In this article I pinpoint twelve areas on which project planners and coordinators could focus in order to ensure that their projects have long-term effects extending well beyond the date when external funding is cut off and high-cost aid personnel are withdrawn. I have taken most of my examples from the Sierra Leone Key English Language Teaching (KELT) Project, which I coordinated from 1984 to 1987. This project, set up in 1981 with assistance from the Overseas Development Administration (ODA) and the British Council, ended in July1987. The main aim of the project was to improve the quality of English teaching at primary level in Sierra Leone through pre-service teacher education in the country's five primary teachers'colleges and in-service teacher education at local level. One of my major concerns was to ensure that the considerable investment of time and money made by the British Council and ODA was safeguarded, and that after July 1987 ELT activity in these areas continued to promote dynamic, progressive change.

Twelve tips

1   Involve local participants at all stages of the innovation process.

Change is often best initiated by local personnel themselves. If a project in syllabus design or materials production is to succeed in the long term, local participants must be involved at all stages in the process, from any initial 'consciousness-raising' exercises, through writing and editing, to evaluation and final revision. In Sierra Leone a new teachers' college ELT syllabus and twenty units of supporting materials for lecturers and students were produced at a series of five workshops held over a period of two and a half years. This might seem an inordinately long time, but the outcome has been that lecturers view the finished product, however imperfect or apparently dated it might seem to an outside observer, as their own work. They thus have a stake in its success, and are far more likely to want to promote and develop it, with suitable adaptations and additions to suit their individual circumstances, than if a team of writers had produced a professionally more polished and up-to-date piece of work to be imposed from the top down.

2   Leave behind materials which local personnel can utilize.

People come and go, but print lives on. In most developing countries print materials are hard to come by, expensive, and often not entirely relevant to local circumstances. We can gain the maximum mileage from high-cost expertise by ensuring that project personnel create appropriate and relevant print materials which will be left behind when the 'experts' leave. In Sierra Leone, a package of 16 topic-based instructors' notes and supporting materials for in-service workshops has been created. The package was largely the work of VSO and CSO volunteers attached to the project, along with their Sierra Leonean counterparts. Each unit was edited by a KELT lecturer, and the whole package is currently being revised and re-issued. It is anticipated that this package will provide source materials for local teacher supervisors and others involved in primary level INSET (for example, Peace Corps volunteers) for at least the next ten years.

3   Provide adequate incentives.

In most developing countries, teaching, as in Britain, is a low-status, low-paid profession. We can help to ensure that loyalty and morale are maintained by providing incentives. In Sierra Leone a major incentive has been the opportunity for further study overseas. While it is important to realize that awards for training are allocated on merit and are necessary for the success of the project - they are not *just* an incentive - the opportunity afforded to the best performers ensures that other teachers perform at their best, in the hope of being themselves selected for further training. ODA has sponsored several lecturers from each primary teachers' college for diploma courses, and thirteen teachers supervisors for short, three-month courses in the U.K. In addition, a few lecturers have been sent for MA courses, and teacher supervisors for one-year diplomas in ELT. Higher qualifications automatically guarantee a higher salary, so the incentive is financial as well as purely academic or educational. Other incentives in Sierra Leone have included the provision of t-shirts with a printed motif for teacher supervisors, and files for college lecturers. Other possibilities might include the provision of project pens and pencils, or presentation packs of resource books for teacher supervisors.

4   Secure internal resources for maintenance.

If project activity is to continue beyond the formal end of external input, internal/local resources for maintenance must be guaranteed. This is something which project planners might consider writing into bilateral agreements from the start of a project. Local costs saved by the departure of foreign experts, for example the costs of salaries or housing for volunteers, could be diverted to provide spare parts or fuel for transport, or paper and ink for materials production. It is vital that a Ministry or Institute of Education which inherits a project should include the project in its forward financial planning and make adequate budgetary provision for continued activity.

5   Provide on-going support for replication and further development.

There is an unfortunate tendency for projects to be totally abandoned by external aid agencies once expatriate or volunteer personnel have been withdrawn. However, it is essential that provision should be made for replication and further development so that a dynamic process of change continues to be fostered. Within the ODA-funded KELT scheme, provision exists for U.K. personnel funded by ODA and the British Council to run a continuing programme of education seminars. This arrangement worked well in Tanzania, where prior to and following the withdrawal of ODA-funded lecturers from primary teachers' colleges, a series of visits by a colleague from the Leeds Overseas Education Unit led to the production of a manual on reading for college tutors, with an accompanying students' text. The manual embodies a highly prescriptive approach with an overt teacher-training function. There is also a need for the provision of funds to reprint and revise materials produced during the life of a project (for example, Foston 1985), or which are produced by local personnel after the formal end of the project.

6   Involve all interested parties.

Towards the end of a project, it would seem wise to adopt an octopus-like approach, giving as many different parties and agencies as possible an interest in its success. In Sierra Leone, the KELT project has fostered close ties with VSO, CUSO, the Peace Corps, UNDP/UNESCO and IDA. A policy of openness and involvement helps to guard against petty jealousies and territorial disputes which can jeopardise even the best-run schemes. It also ensures that, if the primary donor agency is unable or unwilling to put in further funding beyond the agreed formal ending of the project, there are other sources to which to turn. In Sierra Leone on the withdrawal of the majority of VSO volunteers from the project in 1984, ODA donated their motorcycles to the Ministry of Education for use by Sierra Leonean counterparts – but was not able to fund running costs. However, CUSO, which had earlier provided two of the volunteers attached to the project, provided funds for petrol, oil, and spare parts from 1984 to 1987, and thus kept the wheels turning.

7   Create a nexus of counterparts.

The philosophy of most aid donors involves a theory of 'counterparting', under which the host country or institution provides counterpart staff to be trained, either on-the-job or overseas, and who will eventually assume the responsibilities of the expatriate 'experts'. However, to place undue reliance on one or two individuals can lead to acute embarrassment if those identified for training and eventual succession are promoted or transferred. It would seem wise, therefore, to create a nexus of counterparts who together can assume the responsibilities of the foreign experts. In Sierra Leone, such an approach has led to the KELT Coordinator working closely with an official from the Ministry of Education at in-service level, and with a different official from the Institute of Education at pre-service level. Other officials, however, have been involved in the running of workshops and seminars at both levels and are involved in coordinating and advisory committees for the planning and supervision of project activities. In the sixteen districts, teacher supervisors conduct in-service workshops, one supervisor per district, and virtually all members of college English Departments are involved with teaching the new syllabus. Thus a substantial network of 'counterparts' has been created, without undue reliance on any single individual.

8   Invoke the principle of gradually diminishing control.

Towards the formal end of a project, the 'experts' must repress the instinct to take charge and direct operations. Local personnel must be allowed to assume responsibility and take decisions on the future direction and day-to-day running of the project, even if this appears (at least from some points of view) to lead to some fall-off in efficiency or focus. After all, if local staff cannot be entrusted with responsibility while the 'experts' are still around, they are even less likely to perform effectively once the last 'expert' has stepped onto the plane home. Project-planning sessions can be handed over to a local committee, and local officials can assume responsibility for filling in requests for support or compiling reports on project activities. In his or her last few months at post, a project leader should be able to assume the role of a 'fly on the wall', stepping in only if things appear to be going badly wrong.

9   Establish forecasting and reporting procedures and feedback loops.

Teachers often get impatient with apparently unnecessary bureaucracy, but one important aspect of maintenance involves the filing of forecasts of activity, submitting of reports on work done, and supplying feedback to the centre on methods and materials. In Sierra Leone, teacher supervisors complete forecasts at the start of each term, detailing anticipated workshops and follow-up visits to schools. Then at the end of the term, they file a separate report on the workshops actually done during the term. Having become accustomed to this procedure, it is to be hoped that they are continuing with such routines beyond the formal end of the project, as the local coordinator is likely to be considerably less mobile than the former expatriate coordinator. College lecturers are encourage to complete an evaluation questionnaire after each unit tyey have taught. This enables information to be gathered for any later revision of the materials, and also provides a check on what is actually being taught.

10   Ensure that examinations fit with revised syllabuses and materials.

In the developing world especially, examinations have a tremendous influence over what is taught and how learning and teaching take place. The most innovative and up-to-date curriculum packages will not succeed unless assessment and examination procedures and formats are correspondingly revised. All too frequently, it is the examinations cart which leads the curriculum horse. It is therefore absolutely vital to the success of any syllabus or materials design project to ensure that examinations are modified to fit the revised curriculum. In Sierra Leone, some progress has been made towards this goal: a national seminar on Assessment was held in February 1986, and a seminar specifically on ELT assessment was projected for early 1988. The format of the Teacher's Certificate examination is gradually being modified to reflect the new syllabus and materials, and it is anticipated that by July 1988 external final examinations will be set wholly on the new syllabus for the first time.

11   Replace high-cost 'experts' by low-cost volunteers.

Once highly qualified, widely experienced paid and highly paid 'experts' are due to leave, local personnel may feel abandoned and powerless in the face of apparently insurmountable problems. One way of dealing with this is to replace the experts with qualified and enthusiastic volunteers for a specifically planned period.   In Sierra Leone, the phased withdrawal of experts began in 1985,and a KELT lecturer at one of the teachers' colleges was replaced by an experienced and competent volunteer who will be withdrawn in July 1988.

12   Expect some loss of momentum but retain an optimistic attitude.

The withdrawal of external financial and human resources can lead to some loss of momentum and a fall-off in the level of project activity. This is only to be expected. Frequently during the closing stages of a project, the planner or adviser is sure to wonder if he or she has been building a house of cards. Donors may be reluctant to continue to support the project financially because they fear that there may not be the same degree of checks and balances within the system. Advisers may feel that it is useless to try yet again to extract the promise of financial support from a hard-pressed Ministry because they have tried many times before and failed each time. Counterparts may be apprehensive about losing the back-up and support provided by the external donor to the experts, once these have left. However, a positive, optimistic attitude will often produce the required result. This is perhaps the equivalent of the 'Hawthorne effect'. If you believe a project can succeed without you, it will, and *vice versa*.

REFERENCES

1 Kargbo, M.S., British Foreign Policy and the Conflict in Sierra Leone, 1991-2001, Peter Lang, 2006. p 85

2 Hunter T, Micropolitical Issues in ELT Project Implementation, in Alderson, J.S. (Ed) The Politics of Language Education: Individuals and Institutions Multilingual Matters, 2009. p67

3. Hayes, A. Planning a Project: The KELT Project, Sierra Leone in Brumfit, C.J. Language Teaching Projects for the Third World ELT Documents 16, Pergamon Press, Oxford, 1983.

4. ibid p 15

5. ibid p 17

6. ibid p 18

7. Lutz J. and Devi, L. Nutrition education at the Primarv-school level: the Bunumbu project - a case study in Nutrition Education: Case Study Experiences in Schools, UNESCO Division of Science Technical and Vocational Education Paris 1983 p 21

8. Hayes, A, ibid p 27

9. Stevens, S, What Life Has Taught Me: the Autobiography of President Siaka Stevens of Sierra Leone. Kensal Press, Bourne End, 1984

10. Seguin, X, Once Upon a Time Sierra Leone... and a President Called Siaka Stevens, ABC/Group Media International, Paris, 1984

11. ibid p 5

12. ibid pp 8-9

13. ibid p18

14. ibid p 23

15. ibid p 31

16. ibid pp 46-48

17. Joy, E., Green Oranges on Lion Mountain, London, Eye Books 2004 p14

18. Downloaded on 14.1.2018 from https://en.wikipedia.org/wiki/2007_Paramount_Airlines_Mil_Mi-8_crash

19. Downloaded on 11.2.2018 from https://www.tripadvisor.co.uk/Restaurant_Review-g293833-d1444174-Reviews-Alex_s_Beach_Bar_and_Restaurant-Freetown_Western_Area.html

20. Downloaded on 11.2.2018 from http://wikieducator.org/Tech-MODE_in_Sierra_Leone

21. Millar, G., An Ethnographic Approach to Peacebuilding Routledge, 2014, pp 33-34

22. Downloaded on 15.1.2018 from https://en.wikipedia.org/wiki/Krio_language

23. Downloaded on 15.1.2018 from https://en.wikipedia.org/wiki/Cane_rat

24. Millar, G., ibid p 34

25. ibid, p 34

26. ibid p 35

27. Downloaded on 16.1.2018 from https://www.power-technology.com/projects/bumbuna-station/

28. Downloaded on 16.1.2018 from
http://www.hydroworld.com/articles/2017/08/joule-africa-sierra-leone-sign-25-year-ppa-for-50-mw-bumbuna-expansion.html

29. Downloaded on 16.1.2018 from
http://www.nytimes.com/1982/05/03/world/around-the-world-sierra-leone-voids-some-election-returns.html

30. Downloaded on 16.1.2018 from
https://en.wikipedia.org/wiki/Sierra_Leonean_parliamentary_election,_1982

31. Downloaded on 17.1.2018 from
https://englishagenda.britishcouncil.org/sites/default/files/attachments/f044_elt-56_the_development_of_elt_-_the_dunford_seminars_1978-1993_v3.pdf

32. Downloaded on 17.1.2018 from
https://awoko.org/2015/11/18/sierra-leone-news-mp-cries-for-govt-help-to-kurubonla/

33. Reese, M.R. The Unknown Origins of the Ancient Nomoli figures. Downloaded on 18.1.2018 from
http://www.ancient-origins.net/artifacts-other-artifacts/unknown-origins-mysterious-nomoli-figures-002513?nopaging=1

34. Downloaded on 17.01.2018 from
http://www.lakkabeachresort.com/

35. Downloaded on 17.01.2018 from
https://www.theguardian.com/travel/2011/dec/05/best-africa-beaches

36. Knight J, et al., Sierra Leone. Bradt Travel Guides, Chalfont St Peter, 2018 p 259

37. ibid, p 259

38. Downloaded on 18.1.2018 from
https://en.wikipedia.org/wiki/Ndogboyosoi_War

39. Downloaded on 23.1.2018 from
https://en.wikipedia.org/wiki/Bonthe_District

40. Downloaded on 23.1.2018 from
https://pjhap.wordpress.com/category/history/houses/

41. Downloaded on 23.1.2018 from
http://www.aljazeera.com/indepth/inpictures/2015/07/sierra-leone-layers-history-150714082258599.html

42. Downloaded on 26.1.2018 from
https://en.wikipedia.org/wiki/Ahmed_S%C3%A9kou_Tour%C3%A9

43. Downloaded on 28.1.2018 from
http://www.nytimes.com/1985/12/06/world/britain-confirms-its-plan-to-quit-a-harmfully-politicalized-unesco.html

44. ibid

45. Downloaded on 28.1.2018 from
http://web.warwick.ac.uk/fac/soc/CELTE/eltarchive/Archive/overview_bycountry.php

46. Downloaded on 28.1.2018 from
https://ia801404.us.archive.org/0/items/ERIC_ED358711/ERIC_ED358711.pdf
British Council Dunford House Seminar Report, 1989. Originally published as Woods , P. Pulling Out of a Project: Twelve Tips for Project Planners, in ELTJ Journal Vol 42/3, Oxford, OUP, 1988

47. National Curriculum Development Centre, Institute of Education, Sierra Leone. Report of KELT Seminar on Literature Teaching in Teachers' Colleges, March 16-April 3 1987. Freetown, 1987 (mimeo). p 1.

48. ibid, p 97

49. Downloaded on 29.1.2018 from
https://en.wikipedia.org/wiki/Lansana_Cont%C3%A9

50. Downloaded on 29.1.2018 from
https://en.wikipedia.org/wiki/Moussa_Dadis_Camara

ABOUT THE AUTHOR

Following a year as a VSO volunteer in Nigeria, Paul Woods taught English and trained teachers in Brunei and Tanzania, then spent six years as a primary teacher trainer and British Council KELT Professional Coordinator in Sierra Leone, where he met his wife Fatmata (Fanta). After Sierra Leone he worked for the British Council's Overseas Career Service in a variety of posts. He has two grown up children and a Labrador retriever named Luna. At the last count he had visited 117 different countries.

Proof

Made in the USA
Columbia, SC
03 February 2018